# SpringerBriefs in Economics



For further volumes:
http://www.springer.com/series/8876

Carol Yeh-Yun Lin · Leif Edvinsson
Jeffrey Chen · Tord Beding

# National Intellectual Capital and the Financial Crisis in Australia, Canada, Japan, New Zealand, and the United States

Springer

Carol Yeh-Yun Lin
Dept. of Business Administration
National Chengchi University
Taipei
Taiwan

Jeffrey Chen
Accenture
Chicago
Illinois
USA

Leif Edvinsson
Universal Networking Intellectual Capita
Norrtalje
Sweden

Tord Beding
TC-Growth AB
Karlstad
Sweden

ISSN 2191-5504
ISSN 2191-5512 (electronic)
ISBN 978-1-4614-9307-5
ISBN 978-1-4614-9308-2 (eBook)
DOI 10.1007/978-1-4614-9308-2
Springer New York Heidelberg Dordrecht London

Library of Congress Control Number: 2013950095



Printed on acid-free paper

Springer is part of Springer Science+Business Media (www.springer.com)

# Foreword 1

The economic crisis is a consequence of many parallel factors which are all related to globalization and digitalization. My main concern, assessing this in more detail from the European perspective, is that revolutionary global forces have not been taken early nor seriously enough by most national and regional decision makers. The Heads of European States and Governments have once again recalled the importance of fiscal consolidation, structural reform, and targeted investment to put Europe back on the path of smart, sustainable, and inclusive growth. The main question is how capable and ready are the national governments of tackling the complex and manifold issues of crises and of renewing even radically many of our public and private structures and processes.

The first basic requirement is that all the European Union member states remain fully committed to taking the actions required at the national level to achieve the objectives of the Europe 2020 Strategy. The second basic requirement is that the national and regional governments, as well as the people, are ready for radical changes. This booklet, and the other 11 booklets by the experienced authors, focus on national intellectual capital and give necessary insights and facts for us, the readers and especially for our in-depth systemic thinking of the interrelationships of NIC and economic recovery.

How should the national and regional decision makers tackle the existing knowledge of intangible capital? The focus needs to be more on the bottom-up approach stressing the developments on local and regional levels. I highlight our recent statements by the EU Committee of the Regions. The key priorities are to get more innovations out of research and to encourage mindset change towards open innovation.

The political decision makers are finally aware that the traditional indicators created for and used in industrial production cannot be applied to a knowledge-intensive, turbulent, and innovativeness-based global enterprise environment. Indicators that perceive the intangible dimensions of competitiveness—knowledge capital, innovation knowledge, and anticipation of the future—have been developed around the world, but their use has not yet become established in practice. This booklet accelerates the development and the use of these indicators.

This helps the local and regional, as well as central, governments in taking brave leaps forward on a practical level—giving greater ownership and involving all the stakeholders. This means the need of actions towards increasing the structural and relational capital of regions, both internally in communities of practice and in collaboration with others.

The new generation innovation activities are socially motivated, open and collectively participated, complex and global by nature. The regions need to move towards open innovation, within a human-centered vision of partnerships between public and private sector actors, with universities playing a crucial role.

Regions should be encouraged to develop regional innovation platforms, which act as demand-based service centers and promote the use of international knowledge to implement the Europe 2020 Strategy, smart specialization and European partnerships according to the interests and needs of regions. For this to happen, we need to apply the new dynamic understanding of regional innovation ecosystems, in which companies, cities, and universities as well as other public and private sector actors (the "Triple Helix") learn to work together in new and creative ways to fully harness their innovative potential.

New innovative practices do not come about by themselves. One major potential is the use of public procurement. The renewing of the European wide rules must increase the strategic agility and activities of municipalities and other public operators as creators of new solutions. Especially the execution of pre-commercial procurement should be reinforced even more in combination with open innovation to speed up the green knowledge society development, i.e., for common reusable solutions in creating the infrastructures and services modern real-world innovation ecosystems are built upon. Conditions must be created that also allow for extensive development projects which address complex societal challenges and which take the form of risk-taking consortia.

One of our working instruments within the Committee of the Regions is the Europe 2020 Monitoring Platform, which broadly reviews and reflects the opinions and decisions on regional level all around Europe. It gives a flavor of cultural and other socioeconomic differences inside the EU. This brings an important perspective to the intellectual capital, namely the values and attitudes needed for citizens supporting policymakers on appropriate long-term investments and policies.

Emphasizing the importance of these issues, decision-makers in all countries and regions worldwide need a deep and broad understanding of the critical success factors affecting the national intellectual capital. With all the facts and frames for thinking, this booklet gives a valuable insight in today's challenges.

Markku Markkula
Advisor to the Aalto University Presidents
Member of the EU Committee of the Regions
Former Member of the Parliament of Finland

# Foreword 2

Financial crisis—words very much heard today. What is it about, actually, and how to get a grip on what we experience today? The booklet gives an important insight on the factors affecting competitiveness and productivity in modern knowledge society. We need to see beyond the obvious, and have increasingly "qualified guesses" because the character of the society and industry has fundamentally changed.

What is very important to notice is the shift towards intangible value creation beyond the deterministic phenomena we saw very clearly in the industrial era. Cost drivers were the important ones throughout the industry. Mass production, bigger is better; very traditional productivity factors, was the mantra.

However, the production picture is changing. Increasingly value is created by the intangibles, often services related to the tangible components, and even totally in immaterial value creation, where perceptions and expectations determine the market value of the "extended product." We also see rapid change in organizational forms, a new type of entrepreneurship growing besides the traditional industry clusters, and also smart specialization of regions and countries.

This also means that there will be clearly different and complementary roles of the actors in innovation and value creation ecosystems. Large companies, small ones, and even microenterprises together with the public sector are traditionally seen as the active partners in such innovation environments. The real issue in the dynamic markets, however, is that the end users are increasingly to be taken on board as *active subjects* for innovation, and not merely treated as objects or customers. Markets need to be shaped and created in a much more dynamic way than ever before. Open innovation beyond cross-licensing includes the societal capital as an important intangible engine for productivity growth. Innovation happens only when the offering meets the demand. Otherwise we can only speak about inventions or ideas…

We need to have a closer look at the intellectual capital and the different factors within it when we design our policy approaches. Short-term investments in process capital (infrastructures) and market capital seem to be very important for the manufacturing base as such, but at the same time measures for longer-term intellectual capital development and efficiency need to be taken.

The *structure* and the open *processes* related to intangible capital and knowledge pools is increasingly important. For sustainable long-term development, both the *human capital and renewal capital are crucial*, as they are directly related to the innovation capability of the region. The correlation between these factors and the GDP growth is undisputable. In knowledge-intense industries, talent attracts talent, and the connectivity that modern ICT provides makes this talent pool fluid across disciplines, organizations, and geographical settings. It is imperative to modernize the innovation systems enabling the full dynamics needed for success in knowledge intense industries, beyond the traditional boundaries.

Measuring the performance of innovation systems becomes increasingly complex due to the mash-up of different disciplines and having new types of actors and interactions between them. Hence, the importance of analysis of the various components of the national intellectual capital (and equally on national innovation capability) as done in this booklet cannot be underestimated when making qualified guesses for operational choices to create functioning innovation ecosystems. The only thing predictable in true innovation is the unpredictability and the surprises. The role of the public sector is to drive strategy and measures enabling the unpredictable, and to catalyze a fluid, seamless, and frictionless innovation system to grow, with strong interplay with the surrounding society.

We need to have the courage to experiment, prototype in real world settings, have all stakeholders involved to find and remove the friction points of innovation, and achieve sustainable innovation ecosystems for knowledge-intense products and services.

I wish you an interesting read with this mind-opening report.

Bror Salmelin
Advisor, Innovation Systems
European Commission
DG CONNECT

# Foreword 3

The 2008 global financial crisis hit the whole world with unprecedented speed, causing widespread financial panic. Consumer confidence dropped to the lowest level since the Great Depression. Taiwan, with an export-dependent economy, was seriously impacted by the crisis and the unemployment rate hiked while household consumption levels dropped. At the onset of the financial crisis, Professor Lin was the Dean of Student Affairs here at National Chengchi University in Taipei, Taiwan. She was the dean in charge of financial aid and student loans and thus saw first-hand the direct impact the financial crisis had upon our students. The crisis was so devastating that Professor Lin, along with the university, was compelled to launch several new initiatives to raise money and help students weather the difficult times.

I am very glad that she took this painful experience to heart and set herself upon the task of investigating the impact of the crisis; trying to look into the causes and consequences for policy implications, not only for Taiwan but for an array of 48 countries. In particular, she approaches the crisis from the perspective of "national intellectual capital," which is very important in today's knowledge-driven economy.

Taiwan is an example of a knowledge economy and has enjoyed the fame of being referred to as a "high-tech island." Without an abundance of natural resources, Taiwan's hardworking and highly educated population is the single most precious resource that the island has. Acknowledging the value of such human resources and intellectual capital, we established the Taiwan Intellectual Capital Research Center (TICRC) under my leadership in 2003. Ever since then, Taiwan's government has continuously funded the university to conduct relevant research projects aimed at enhancing the intellectual capital of Taiwan. Having been thus endowed with the responsibility of nourishing future leaders in the public and private sectors, we have focused on building up our strength in innovation, entrepreneurship, and technology management-related research and education.

To enhance intellectual capital research, we recently formed a joint team of professors for a 4-year project in order to leverage their respective research capabilities. Through this project we hope to provide policy suggestions for the government by exploring the creativity, innovation, and intellectual capital at national, regional, city, and county levels. The goal is to come up with an intangible assets agenda for Taiwan's future sustainability. Professor Lin is an integral member of this research team.

Following her 2011 book *National Intellectual Capital: A Comparison of 40 Countries*, this booklet series is Professor Lin's second attempt at presenting her research, conducted under the sponsorship of TICRC, to international readers. As the Founding Director of TICRC and her President, I am honored to give a brief introduction of the value of this booklet series.

In comparison to her 2011 book, this series increased the number of countries studied to 48 and particularly focuses on the impact of intellectual capital on the 2008 global financial crisis. Rarely has an economic issue been systematically studied from the view point of intangible assets, particularly at such a large scale of 48 countries. The research results show without a doubt that national intellectual capital is indeed an important economic development enhancer. In particular, the fact that countries with higher national intellectual capital experienced faster recoveries from the 2008 financial crisis provides a strong message for the policy makers.

In addition to providing insights to national policy, the booklet also summarizes the background of each country before the crisis, the key events during the crisis, economic development afterwards, and future prospects and challenges. Each volume affords readers a holistic picture of what happened in each country in an efficient manner. The linkage between national intellectual capital and this financial crisis also provides a different perspective of the crisis.

We are happy that Professor Lin continues to share her valuable research results with international readers. I sincerely hope that her insights can garner more attention concerning the benefits of developing national intellectual capital for the well-being of every nation.

Se-Hwa Wu
Professor, Graduate Institute of Technology and Innovation Management
President, National Chengchi University, Taipei, Taiwan

# Preface 1

There are "mounting risks of a breakup of the Euro zone." Such comments are frequent today on how the European leaders are handling the escalating crisis and its potential impact on non-European countries. However, few leaders, reporters, or researchers are actually addressing the situation of national intellectual capital (NIC) and its signals. In addition to the financial crisis, is there an emerging NIC crisis as well? Why is it emerging? How should policy makers think about NIC? In what way does it need specific attention? When will the outcome and impact of taken NIC policy steps be realized?

In the midst of the European crisis, there are national interventions to address the issues mentioned above. In leading economical nations, the investments going into intangibles now exceeds tangibles, and is positively correlated to income per capita. However, these still do not show up clearly in national mapping as well as policy making insights. Therefore, the New Club of Paris is focusing the knowledge agenda setting for countries on Societal Innovation (see www.new-club-of-paris.org).

Chairman Ben Bernanke of the U.S. Federal Reserve was addressing some of these same aspects in a key note speech in May 2011 hosted by Georgetown University: http://www.icapitaladvisors.com/2011/05/31/bernanke-on-intangible-capital/. OECD and the World Bank are developing NIC statistics, often based on the model from Corrado-Hultén. Japan has been developing both NIC and Intangible Assets (IA) at METI for some time now. Their research on IC/IA has resulted in a National IA Week with various key stakeholders such as government agencies, universities, stock exchange, and enterprises. Japan is so far the only country in the world to hold such activities, and they have been doing so for the last 8 years. Australia, Singapore, South Korea, and China are currently undertaking various NIC initiatives. Other countries are also becoming more and more aware of NIC, with policy rhetoric centered on innovation, education, R&D, and trade. Despite this, the map for a more justified NIC navigation has been missing.

This booklet highlights NIC development for a number of countries, based on 48 different indicators, aggregated into four major NIC components of human capital, market capital, process capital, and renewal capital. The model here is a refined and verified statistical model in comparison to the Corrado–Hultén model. We call it the L–E–S model after the contributors Lin–Edvinsson–Stahle. Based on a deeper understanding and the timeline pattern it sets forth, this model will add to a better NIC navigation, not to mention knowledge agenda setting for countries.

Upon looking at a global cluster NIC map, it is evident that the top leading countries seem to be small countries, especially Singapore, the Nordic countries, Hong Kong, and Taiwan. For the USA, Finland, and Sweden, around 50 % or more of its economical growth is related to NIC aspects. Sweden, Finland, Switzerland, the USA, Israel, and Denmark are strongly influenced in its GDP growth by focusing on Renewal Capital.

It might be possible that we will see a clearer map of the NIC ecosystem and drivers for wealth emerge in the extension of this ongoing unique research of NIC. This booklet will present an NIC map for various clusters of countries. It can be used for bench marking as well as bench learning for policy prototyping. The starting point is awareness and thinking of NIC, and its drivers for economic results. Based on this more refined navigation, NIC metrics can be presented.

Deeper understanding will emerge from this research, such as the scaling up of limited skilled human capital in one nation by using the globalized broadband technologies for migration and flow of knowledge (such as telemedicine or mobile banking in Africa). This is also referred to as the IC multiplier. It might also be the way the old British Commonwealth was constructed, but without the IC taxonomy. In modern taxonomy, might it be the shaping of NIC alliances for the migration and flow of IC between nations?

Another understanding that might emerge for policy making is the issue of employment versus unemployment. The critical understanding will be deployment of IC drivers. This will require another networked workforce of value networkers on a global scale, such as volunteering software and apps developers. However, such volunteers do not show up in traditional statistics for the mapping on behalf of policymakers.

On another level, there might be clear gap analyses between nations to support the vision process of a nation. On a deeper level, it is also a leadership responsibility to address the gap of NIC positions versus potential positions. Such a gap is in fact a liability to the citizens, to be addressed in due time.

This will take us to the need for the continuous renewal of social systems. The so called Arab Spring is explained by some as resulting from three drivers: lack of renewal of social systems, Internet, and soccer as cross class interaction space. The lack of social renewal and innovation is most likely critical early warning signals. For Greece, we can see that such a tipping point occurred back in 1999.

On a global scale, we might see that the concern for the Euro zone crisis should and can be explained by a deeper and supplementary understanding of National Intellectual Capital, in addition to financial capital. Hence, we need to refine our NIC understanding, NIC mapping, NIC metrics, and NIC organizational constructs into societal innovation for the benefit of wealth creation of subsequent generations.

Leif Edvinsson
The World's First Professor of Intellectual Capital
Chairman and Co-founder of New Club of Paris

# Preface 2

Our first book *National Intellectual Capital: A Comparison of 40 Countries* was published in early 2011, at a time when the 2008 global financial crisis had been declared when the European region was still plagued with sovereign debt problems. Before we finalized the book, we were able to retrieve some of our raw data concerning the troubled countries, such as Greece, Iceland, Ireland, Portugal, and Spain. The results of our analysis based on data spanning 1995 to 2008 revealed some early warning signs of the financial turmoil in those countries. In my preface of that book, I mentioned that the warning signs might reveal only the tip of an iceberg. At that time, my co-author, Professor Edvinsson and I decided to do a follow-up study to trace the development of national intellectual capital (NIC) in as many countries as possible, particularly through the lens of the 2008 global financial crisis. This 12 booklet series is the result of that determination.

The 2008 global financial crisis came with unexpected speed and had such a widespread effect that it surprised many countries far from the epicenter of the initial U.S. sub-prime financial problem, geographically and financially. According to reports, no country was immune to the impact of this financial crisis. Such development clearly signifies how closely connected the world has become and the importance of having a global interdependent view. By reporting what happened during 2005–2010 in 48 major countries throughout the world, this booklet series serves the purpose of uncovering national problems before the crisis, government coping strategies, stimulus plans, potential prospects and challenges of each individual country, and the interdependence between countries. The 6 years of data allow us to compare NIC and economic development crossing before, during, and after the financial crisis. They are handy booklets for readers to have a quick yet overall view of countries of personal interest. The list of 48 countries in 11 clusters is provided in the appendix of each booklet.

Searching for financial crisis-related literature for 48 countries is itself a very daunting task, not to mention summarizing and analyzing it. For financial crisis-related literature, we mainly relied on the reports and statistics of certain world organizations, including OECD, World Bank, United Nations, International Monetary Fund (IMF), European Commission Office, the US Congressional Research Service, the U.S. Central Intelligence Agency, and International Labor Office (ILO).

Some reliable research centers such as the National Bureau of Economic Research in the U.S., World Economic Forum, the Heritage Foundation in the U.S., and government websites from each country were also our sources of information. Due to the requirement of more update and comprehensive information, we were not able to use as much academic literature as we would have liked, because it generally covers a very specific topic with time lag and with research methods not easily comprehended by the general public. Therefore, we had to resort to some online news reports for more current information.

In the middle of 2012, the lasting financial troubles caused the European economy to tilt back into a recession, which also slowed down economic growth across the globe. However, almost 4 years have passed since the outbreak of the global financial crisis in late 2008; it is about time to reflect on what happened and the impact of the financial crisis. By comparing so many countries, we came to a preliminary conclusion that countries with faster recovery from the financial crisis have higher national intellectual capital than those with slower recovery. In other words, countries that rebounded fast from the crisis generally have solid NIC fundamentals, including human capital, market capital, process capital, and renewal capital. We also found that higher the NIC, higher is the GDP per capita (ppp). This booklet series provides a different perspective to look beyond the traditional economic indicators for national development.

In an era when intangible assets have become a key competitive advantage, investing in national intellectual capital development is investing in future national development and well-being.

Enjoy!

Carol Yeh-Yun Lin
Professor, Dept. of Business Administration
National Chengchi University, Taiwan
Taiwan Intellectual Capital Research Center (TICRC)

# Executive Summary

*The soundness of national governance was tested in the global financial crisis, which reflects the development of national intangible assets.*

How can national intellectual capital (NIC) act as a policy guideline for national well-being? One of the key causes of the financial crisis was the failure of conventional financial metrics and accounting systems to detect potential risks due to non-transparent information disclosure. Our earlier national intellectual capital (NIC) research revealed warning signs of impending financial crisis for Greece, Iceland, and Ireland. Such findings indicate that NIC, albeit intangible, can provide valuable insights into risk control and strategy formulation. This booklet looks at the connections between the financial crisis and NIC development for Australia, Canada, Japan, New Zealand, and the USA.

In particular, this report attempts to answer the following questions: How did these countries weather the 2008 global financial crisis? Why were Australia, Canada, and New Zealand more resilient to the financial shock than other advanced countries? What are the NIC profiles of these countries? What role has NIC played in the national development of these countries?

Data covering 2005–2010 for 48 countries indicate that *the higher the NIC, the higher is the GDP per capita (ppp)*, accentuating the value of NIC as a driver in major countries throughout the world. *For the six-year average of NIC rankings among 48 countries, Australia ranks 13th, Canada 12th, Japan 15th, New Zealand 21st, and the USA 7th.* In general, these countries are in the second quartile of 48-country NIC, except the USA.

The 2008 financial crisis caused severe impacts across the globe and is considered to be the worst crisis since the Great Depression of the 1930s. The crisis came with unexpected speed and spread into a global economic shock, which resulted in a number of bank failures. During this period, economies worldwide slowed, credits tightened, and international trade declined. In an effort to mitigate the crisis, governments and central banks across the globe responded with unprecedented fiscal stimuli, monetary policy expansions, and institutional bailouts. These measures had their desired impact and the financial crisis was declared over by the end of 2009.

However, the short global recovery in 2010 was overshadowed by the lingering sovereign debt problems in Europe, thus a global economic slowdown recurred in the second half of 2011. Despite the efforts of European leaders to prevent large economies like Italy and Spain from needing bailouts, Spain still asked for external financial assistance in June 2012. Although the global economic outlook for 2013 will be better than that of 2012, growth in most developed countries is still predicted to be weak.

During the financial crisis, Australia, Canada, and New Zealand were relatively resilient compared with other advanced countries for the following reasons.

First, past experience with crises over the last few decades have prompted these countries to improve their financial systems. Second, these countries adopted conservative financial practices that somewhat insulated them from toxic financial products. Third, Australia and New Zealand benefited from China's continuous trading demands even during the financial crisis. Canada's economy was not affected much by the sub-prime mortgage problems of its major trading partner, the USA, mainly because of its conservative financial practices.

In general, relatively sound macroeconomic fundamentals, swift policy responses by their governments, and past experience helped these countries recover from the crisis faster than first expected.

The Global Competitiveness Index ranking (GCI, Fig. 1.1) of Canada and Japan advanced from 14 to 12 and from 12 to 9, respectively in 2011–2012, when compared to their 2005–2006 level. Australia declined from 10 to 20, New Zealand from 16 to 25, and the USA from 2 to 5 with the same comparison. The *real GDP growth* pattern of these countries was largely similar—a drop to negative growth in both 2008 (except Australia) and 2009, and then a rebound to positive growth in 2010. Specifically, Australia experienced less GDP growth fluctuation over the 6 years. Canada and the USA had synchronized development. Japan had the deepest drop in 2009, yet with the strongest rebound in 2010 as well. New Zealand had a relatively flat growth in 2008, 2009, and 2010.

In terms of general *government debt*, Australia and New Zealand carried around 30%, Canada and the USA around 90%, and Japan around 190% of GDP debt in 2010. All the five countries had continuous government debt increase starting from 2008. Aside from GDP growth and government debt, *unemployment* and its social impact is one of the major concerns of the financial crisis. Unemployment rate of all five countries rose starting from 2008, with the USA having the greatest jump, followed by Canada and New Zealand. Australia and Japan were the two countries with the lowest unemployment rate in this group. *Consumer price inflation* (CPI) of these five countries all rose in 2008, dropped drastically in 2009, and then rebounded in 2010. Among them, Canada had the least and the USA had the largest scale fluctuation. Japan had much lower CPI than the other four countries, at around "0," except for fluctuations in 2008 and 2009.

For NIC component capitals, over the six-year time frame of the study (2005–2010), *human capital* (HC) did not vary much among these countries. For *market capital* (MC), Japan and the USA were in the low group, clearly apart from the other three countries. After the financial crisis, all countries (except Japan) had market capital increase. *Process capital* (PC) of these five countries was at the similar level over the 6 years. In terms of PC score, Japan had the lowest score in 2005 and remained the lowest in 2010 in this group. *Renewal capital* (RC) of these five countries was relatively stable over the 6 years. Contrary to market capital, Japan and the USA were in the high renewal capital group, clearly apart from the other three countries. Australia and Canada were in the middle group, with Canada surpassing Australia starting from 2007. New Zealand consistently had the lowest RC in this group. *Financial capital* (based on a 1–10 scale) did not show much difference among these five countries. However, the USA consistently had the highest score and New Zealand the lowest even though the difference was small. For the overall *NIC*, the USA consistently had the highest score and New Zealand the lowest over the 6 years.

The codevelopment pattern of NIC-GDP, HC-GDP, and PC-GDP was largely the same, with the USA at the top, followed closely by Australia and Canada, then Japan, at lastly, New Zealand. The MC-GDP codevelopment was spread out for the five countries. If MC and GDP was divided into high, middle, and low levels (H.M.L), Australia and Canada were at HM (high MC and middle GDP), Japan at LM, New Zealand at HL, and the USA at LH. For RC-GDP codevelopment, Japan was ahead of Australia and Canada in RC. As for long-term NIC (human capital and renewal capital), Japan and the USA were at the top, followed by Australia and Canada together, and then New Zealand. For short-term NIC (market capital and process capital), the five countries were clustered together with Japan and the USA clearly exhibiting lower MC.

For *dynamic NIC ranking* changes in three time periods (2005–2006, 2007–2008, and 2009–2010), the ranking gains represent increasing international competitiveness (among the 48 countries) after the financial crisis. Australia gained the greatest international competitiveness in financial capital after the financial crisis within this group. However, it also experienced a relatively large decline in human capital and renewal capital. Canada gained international competitiveness in renewal capital and NIC after the crisis. Japan lost its international competitiveness in market capital with a relatively large scale and in NIC with a modest scale after the financial crisis. New Zealand gained most international competitiveness in human capital and process capital after the financial crisis. The USA had a modest drop in market capital after the financial crisis.

NIC 3D *trajectory analysis* was conducted to detect the enhancing and impeding factors of each country in reaching a targeted GDP per capita (ppp), benchmarking Norway due to its highest financial performance among the 48 countries. To reach the GDP level of Norway, Japan has the longest distance (−36.07 %) to cover, followed by New Zealand (−28.80 %), Canada (−24.68 %), the USA (−20.37 %), and Australia (−20.15 %). Interestingly, even though New Zealand consistently had the lowest intangible scores in this group, it still has shorter route than Japan to reach Norway's GDP level. A plausible explanation is that Japan has been in a decade-long economic slowdown, whereas New Zealand is a gradually rising country. When benchmarking the financially strong Norway, Japan is in a disadvantageous position. Specifically, the pupil–teacher ratio was a concern for all five countries.

Employee training needs to be improved in each country except Japan, as do R&D related issues. In addition, transparency of government policy requires special attention, except for Australia and New Zealand. Other issues including capital availability and skilled labor also deserve some attention.

As of mid-2013, the world economic recovery was still hampered by the pending financial problems in the Euro zone. However, signs of stronger recovery have surfaced in the USA and economic prospect in Japan has also turned promising with Shinzō Abe's financial relaxing policy. Although these five advanced countries showed their resilience during this financial crisis, challenges still lie ahead as described in Chap. 5.

The 2008 global financial crisis provided an ideal opportunity for nations to examine/renew/innovate the soundness of their economic system and the effectiveness of *national governance related to NIC*. The following implications are drawn from our research findings. Readers can refer to Chap. 5 for the rationale behind these implications.

1. National intellectual capital development goes together with the economic development and should be regarded as an enhancer of economic growth.
2. Wisdom to strike a financial system balance between conservative and liberal, supervision and autonomy, and traditional practice and innovation is important.
3. The effectiveness of stimulus packages will be judged by achieving national long-term goals rather than only the speed of recovery or reduction of the unemployment rate.
4. The soundness of national governance was tested in the global financial crisis, which reflects the development of national intangible assets.
5. Overdependence on single or limited sources of exports for growth will be unsustainable.
6. In addition to monitoring government debt, household debt and its cause should also be reviewed for national health.
7. Advanced countries need to help increase global public good in addition to private good, especially in bad times.
8. Advanced countries should set the model of environmental friendly economic development for developing countries to follow.
9. Observing the national development of Australia and Canada in the immediate future may provide significant implications.
10. Unbalanced NIC development may jeopardize future economic development.

This report shows that Australia needs to pay more attention to its human capital and renewal capital development and its overreliance on China's demands. Canada is improving in its renewal capital and NIC. In addition, its financial sector gained a stronger position in the world financial system after this financial crisis. Japan was hit hard by the crisis and recovered from it with almost 200 % GDP of government debt. However, its private sectors were relatively rich and household savings were high, which gave the government flexibility in financial maneuvering. In addition, Japan's recent relaxing of its financial system has begun to take effect. New Zealand needs to pay special attention to its declining market capital and can strategize its future NIC development to become compatible with other advanced countries. The USA started recovering at a good pace in 2013, mainly because its energy industry is building up steam. In 2009 and 2010, its NIC ranking did not change much compared to its 2005–2010 average. Being the largest economy in the world, the USA has some responsibility to facilitate world recovery from the 2008 global financial crisis.

In the future, there will be a rise in the intangible economy. In July 2013, the U.S. Bureau of Economic Analysis announced that R&D will no longer be treated as a mere expense; it will be categorized on the government's books as an investment (Coy 2013). In an era when the intangible asset has become a key competitive advantage, investing in national intellectual capital development is, in essence, investing in future national development and well-being. National intellectual capital should be nourished from both a local cultural viewpoint and global interconnectivity by social media. Based on emerging new insights of values, societal history, and citizen relationships, a key focus for the future will be on the fusion of national intellectual capital and social service innovation as well as societal innovation, for the enabling of a new social fabric.

# Contents

# List of Figures

# List of Tables

# List of Appendices

# Chapter 1
# Introduction

In April 2013, the International Monetary Fund (IMF 2013) reported that global prospects have improved but the road to recovery in the advanced economies will remain bumpy. World output growth was predicted to reach 3.25 % in 2013 and 4 % in 2014. In the major advanced economies, activity is expected to gradually accelerate, with the United States taking the lead. However, in the Euro area, there remain risks pertaining to adjustment fatigue, insufficient institutional reform, and prolonged stagnation (IMF 2013). With high fiscal deficits and debt, the United States and Japan need to devise and implement fiscal consolidation plans. Nevertheless, policies have supported a modest growth pickup in some emerging market economies and global growth could be stronger if financial conditions continue to improve. In the wake of the 2008 financial crisis, it is valuable to reflect upon what happened during the last few years in order to gain some insights for future preventive actions.

The 2008 global financial crisis is considered by many economists to be the worst one since the Great Depression of the 1930s. The initial US sub-prime mortgage problem that rapidly developed and spread into a global economic shock caught many national leaders by surprise. The spreading financial woes resulted in the failure of a number of financial institutions, first in some advanced countries, and then in developing countries, such as those in Eastern Europe. World political leaders, national ministers of finance, and central bank directors coordinated their efforts to reduce fear, but the crisis continued and eventually led to a global currency crisis. During this period, economies worldwide slowed, credits tightened, international trade declined, and business and consumer confidence eroded with enormous and rapid job losses.

After the full force of the financial crisis hit in October 2008, there was a call in the United States for a hands-off policy in order to let the markets *work themselves out*, in accordance with how capitalism is theoretically supposed to work. Yet, US Federal Reserve Chairman Ben Bernanke believed that such a policy would be catastrophic and urged government intervention. In a statement to Congress, Mr. Bernanke said, "If we let the banking system fail, no one will talk about the

C. Y.-Y. Lin et al., *National Intellectual Capital and the Financial Crisis in Australia, Canada, Japan, New Zealand, and the United States,* SpringerBriefs in Economics,
DOI 10.1007/978-1-4614-9308-2_1, 

Great Depression anymore, because this will be so much worse" (Reavis 2009). As a result of this, the US government decided to take action to prevent such a failure.

Following the lead of the United States, governments and central banks worldwide responded to the international crisis with unprecedented fiscal stimuli, monetary policy expansions, and institutional bailouts in their respective countries. The financial rescue worked and an economic crisis akin to the Great Depression was avoided. In fact, the crisis was declared over by the third quarter of 2009 (Kehoe 2010). Yet while the crisis was officially over, global economic recovery came to a halt from the second half of 2011 as the European debt crisis escalated. As of late 2012, the global economic outlook remains de-synchronized, with a recession across Europe, a modest growth in the United States, and a solid trajectory across Asia.

Financial crises have been a cyclical recurrence in rich and poor countries alike over the past couple of centuries. Each time, the pattern is similar: capital crunch, currency crash, high inflation, high unemployment, undulations in housing and equity prices, and government defaults on international and domestic debts (Reinhart and Rogoff 2009). The source of the problem generally includes improper rules and policies, ineffective governance, failed surveillance systems, and implementation flaws. During the early stages of this financial crisis, management scholars criticized the inability of the traditional accounting systems to reveal the intangibles that explain hidden risks as well as values for proper decision making (Reavis 2009). The above-stated problems are mainly intangible in nature. In line with the importance of the intangibles, intellectual capital (Edvinsson and Malone 1997) advocating the value of human capital, social capital and the like, has gained increasing attention, which explains the value of examining the connection between national intellectual capital (NIC) and the 2008 global financial crisis.

It is our deep belief that NIC, albeit intangible, can provide valuable insights to policy makers regarding future risk control and strategy formulation. Our previous book, *National Intellectual Capital: A Comparison of 40 Countries* (Lin and Edvinsson 2011; www.nic40.org), was born out of this belief and traces the NIC development of 40 countries over a 14-year period from 1995 to 2008. The data analysis presented in our previous work revealed certain warning signs of impending financial crisis for countries such as Greece, Iceland, and Ireland (Lin and Edvinsson 2011, pp. 327–333). As a follow-up study, this booklet series is an attempt to further understand the relationships between the 2008 global financial crisis and NIC development.

The booklet series, in its entirety, will examine the NIC statuses of 48 countries from the period of 2005–2010 to glean new understanding about whether there is a NIC development pattern that distinguishes fast-recovery countries from slow-recovery ones. This is presented through a series of 11 country clusters, with one booklet focusing on one particular cluster. The clusters are determined based on several factors: geographical proximity, geographical size, or the country's phase of economic development. Focusing on one cluster at a time, we probe the areas of concern within a single country and extend them to compare multiple countries to see whether the situation before and after the crisis can be explained by the intangible NIC. Our data come from the well-recognized International Institute for

Management Development (IMD) in Switzerland. The IMD has been publishing yearly rankings of world competitiveness for around two decades. Hopefully, the analysis in this booklet series can provide a different perspective of the financial crisis for future policy implications.

This volume—Vol. 10—will focus on the five advanced countries of Australia, Canada, Japan, New Zealand, and the United States, as they are in similar economic development stages. This makes it easy to compare and examine them as a cluster. In what follows, this booklet provides an economic background to these five countries as a whole before going into each individual country's development. Through this process, the authors hope to paint a general picture of the economic condition and provide a basis for our dataset and analysis in future sections.

Chapter 2 briefly introduces the impact of 2008 financial crisis on the five countries. Chapter 3 discusses the NIC development of these five countries. Chapter 4 describes issues beyond the financial crisis and Chap. 5 concludes with future perspective and policy implications.

## Economic Background

Since the economic history of these five countries goes back centuries, it is impossible to cover the entire spectrum in this work. As such, this background discussion will consider events in the relatively recent history from 2005 onwards that have the most direct impact upon the current economic conditions of each specific country. In addition, particular attention will be given to the 2008 global financial crisis. In doing so, the authors hope that the background, in conjunction with their later data and analysis, will provide a "before, during, and after" picture of what was happening from a macroeconomic and intangible assets viewpoint.

In 2012, these five advanced countries were known for their continuous recovery from the 2008 global financial crisis. To paint a general picture of their global competitiveness in the most recent years and before the financial crisis, we introduce hereunder the Global Competitiveness Index (GCI) published by the World Economic Forum for the reader's reference. This index is relatively robust, as it takes into account the 12 distinct pillars[1] containing basic requirements, efficiency enhancers, and innovation factors that contribute to a nation's overall economic strength. Based upon commonly accepted economic theory, the development of a total of 142 countries was split into three stages in which different factors play the dominant role in determining the outcome of a country's economy. Stage 1, Stage 2, and Stage 3 are respectively characterized by being factor, efficiency, and innovation driven (Schwab 2011). These five countries were all categorized as Stage-3 economies.

[1] The 12 pillars include: institutions, infrastructure, macroeconomic environment, health and primary education, higher education and training, goods market efficiency, labor market efficiency, financial market development, technological readiness, market size, business sophistication, and innovation.

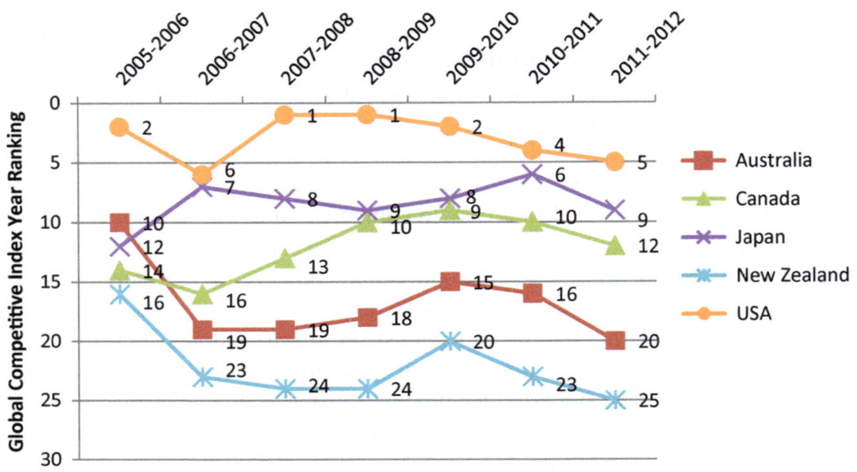


**Fig. 1.1** GCI rankings of the five advanced countries

Plotting each country's annual ranking against a time series of seven periods, Fig. 1.1 displays a rough pictorial overview of their global competitiveness before and after the financial crisis. As an indicator of economic strength in 2011–2012, it can be seen that the United States at #5, Japan #9, Canada #12, Australia #20, and New Zealand #25 are within the top 25 worldwide.

The figure indicates that over the past 7 years, only Canada (from 14 to 12) and Japan (from 12 to 9) have progressed in global competitiveness, when comparing 2005–2006 to 2011–2012. Australia (from 10 to 20) has the greatest ranking slide in 7 years, followed by New Zealand (from 16 to 25), and then the United States (from 2 to 5). Unexpectedly, the GCI ranking of these countries continued to rise during the financial crisis (except the United States), reflecting their resilience. However, their ranking declined in the last two periods (except Japan) rose in 2010–2011. It seems the lasting world economic slowdown had some negative effects on these advanced countries.

In September 2011, the Organisation for Economic Co-operation and Development (OECD) reported that major economies were tilting back into recession as sovereign debt problems continued to ail the Euro zone (Bryant 2011). Concerns about the fiscal and banking problems continue to weigh on the global economic outlook. Economic activity contracted further in Europe (RBA 2012) and the US economy experienced only modest growth. However, much of the developing world had a relatively strong growth.

In January 2012, the World Bank (2012) suggested that the developing countries prepare for further downside risks, as the Euro area debt problems and weakening growth in several big emerging economies were dimming global growth prospects. The World Bank also lowered its growth forecast for 2012 to 5.4% for developing countries and 1.4% for high-income countries (−0.3% for the Euro area), down from its June estimates of 6.2% and 2.7% (1.9% for the Euro area), respectively. It also predicted: “An escalation of the crisis would spare no-one. Developed- and developing-country growth rates could fall by as much or more than in 2008/09.”

In mid-2013, the unemployment rate in Australia jumped to 5.7%, the highest in 4 years and comparable to 5.9% in mid-2009 during the global financial crisis (DJBN 2013). The resource-rich Australia managed to avoid any sharp downturn even amid the crisis due to booming demand for its raw materials from industrializing Asia, especially China. However, China’s recent economic slowdown and the end of its resources boom have resulted in Australian resources industry shedding thousands of workers. Australian central bank has cut interest rates repeatedly to spur weaker sectors of the economy, such as retail and housing construction, by boosting consumer spending (DJBN 2013).

The IMF expected the Canadian economy to grow 1.7% in 2013, slightly stronger than the 1.5% predicted 3 months ago, putting Canada, the second fastest growth country among G-7, on par with the United States and next to Japan. The IMF also predicted Canada’s growth to accelerate to 2.2% in 2014, slower than the 2.4% predicted in April. That leaves Canada also second among the G-7 countries, with the United States displacing Japan from the top spot (Menon 2013).

In mid-2013, the IMF raised its economic growth estimate for Japan to 2.0%, up 0.4 percentage points from its April forecast. The raise reflects the impact of the country’s monetary easing policy, pertaining to the set of monetary, economic, and fiscal measures pursued by Prime Minister Abe to beat deflation and boost Japan’s economy (TJT 2013). However, the IMF cut the Japanese economic growth in 2014 to 1.2%, from 1.4% in its earlier report, predicting a weaker global environment (TJT 2013). The risk of Japan’s sustainability relies on whether the government follows up on its promise to improve the country’s debt-ridden finances and promote structural reforms.

According to the Treasury of New Zealand (2013), its real production GDP growth was forecasted to be 2.5 and 2.4% in the years ending March 2013 and March 2014, respectively, compared with 2.3 and 2.9% of its previous forecast. The 2014 growth rate slows mainly because of the impact of the drought on the economy. Nevertheless, the government predicted that the growth in 2015 and beyond would pick up as business and residential investments rise, in part driven by the Canterbury rebuild and the recovery from the drought. Private consumption was also expected to make a solid contribution to growth in the gross domestic production (GDP) over the forecast period.

During 2013, in the United States, crude-oil and natural-gas production, after declining for two decades, have rocketed with resulting industrial renaissance and have spread its benefits throughout the economy (Colvin 2013). As much of these new productions will be exported, these shrink the trade deficit and bring jobs and GDP growth to the United States. In addition, the 113th US Congress has acted on reforming the tax code by lowering rates and closing loopholes, making Medicare sustainable, and fixing immigration laws to attract and keep the world’s best and most ambitious professionals (Colvin 2013). As a result, the revival of the US economy can be anticipated.

The next chapter will give a brief background and a qualitative analysis of the financial crisis as it relates to these five advanced countries as a whole and individually.

# Chapter 2
# Impact of the 2008 Global Financial Crisis

This global financial crisis is believed to be a direct result of the risky investments in the USA, fueled by a combination of low interest rates, loosening lending standards, growing consumer appetite for debt, and extensive use of securitization. The questionable assessments of credit rating agencies, less disciplined risk management, failure in adequately applying regulations, and the global nature of the financial markets had resulted in the crisis with serious repercussions worldwide, particularly in Europe.

The sign of a financial problem started to surface in 2007; in late 2008, it became clear that the global conditions were much worse than initially envisaged. When businesses ran short of capital, their daily operations were affected, including cessation of production and shedding excessive manpower. When consumers could not get credit or when they lost their jobs, they refrained from spending money and purchasing goods. This cyclical problem affected the real economy, which then developed into the deepest and the most synchronized global crisis seen in the last eight decades. With the two largest import regions, the USA and Europe, in deep financial crises, global international trade dropped drastically, credit tightened, and direct foreign investments were swiftly withdrawn, which resulted in a domino effect of global recession. In the increasingly interconnected world, no country was able to avoid the impact of this financial crisis. By estimation, from January to October 2008, the world stock markets lost 40 % of their value. For the entire world, the estimated US$ 2 trillion total in stimulus packages amounted to approximately 3 % of the world gross domestic product (GDP). This exceeded the call by the International Monetary Fund (IMF) for fiscal stimulus by 2 % of the global GDP.

The USA is the origin of the sub-prime mortgage problem that led to the global financial crisis. The other four advanced countries (Australia, Canada, Japan, and New Zealand) reported in this volume were not immune to this financial turmoil. From its peak in November 2007 to its lows in March 2009, the Australian market declined by 54 %, compared to the peak to trough decline of 57 % in the US market, 60 % in the Japanese market, and 61 % in the European market. At the time of their most recent lows, the Australian stock market had returned to its level seen during mid-2003, the Japanese market was back at levels last seen in 1984, and the US market had fallen back to the levels last seen in the mid-1990s.

C. Y.-Y. Lin et al., *National Intellectual Capital and the Financial Crisis in Australia, Canada, Japan, New Zealand, and the United States,* SpringerBriefs in Economics, DOI 10.1007/978-1-4614-9308-2_2, © The Author(s) 2014

In order to present the impact of the 2008 global financial crisis, this chapter will first graphically compare the overall economic development of the five countries during the time period from 2005 to 2010. Further, it elaborates on the impact of the financial crisis on each country individually in the sequence of Australia, Canada, Japan, New Zealand, and the USA.

This global financial crisis is believed to be a direct result of the risky investments in the USA, fueled by a combination of low interest rates, loosening lending standards, growing consumer appetite for debt, and extensive use of securitization. The questionable assessments of credit rating agencies, less disciplined risk management, failure in adequately applying regulations, and the global nature of the financial markets had resulted in the crisis with serious repercussions worldwide, particularly in Europe.

The sign of a financial problem started to surface in 2007; in late 2008, it became clear that the global conditions were much worse than initially envisaged. When businesses ran short of capital, their daily operations were affected, including cessation of production and shedding excessive manpower. When consumers could not get credit or when they lost their jobs, they refrained from spending money and purchasing goods. This cyclical problem affected the real economy, which then developed into the deepest and the most synchronized global crisis seen in the last eight decades. With the two largest import regions, the USA and Europe, in deep financial crises, global international trade dropped drastically, credit tightened, and direct foreign investments were swiftly withdrawn, which resulted in a domino effect of global recession. In the increasingly interconnected world, no country was able to avoid the impact of this financial crisis. By estimation, from January to October 2008, the world stock markets lost 40 % of their value (Access Economics 2008). For the entire world, the estimated US$ 2 trillion total in stimulus packages amounted to approximately 3 % of the world gross domestic product (GDP). This exceeded the call by the International Monetary Fund (IMF) for fiscal stimulus by 2 % of the global GDP (Nanto, 2009).

The USA is the origin of the sub-prime mortgage problem that led to the global financial crisis. The other four advanced countries (Australia, Canada, Japan, and New Zealand) reported in this volume were not immune to this financial turmoil. From its peak in November 2007 to its lows in March 2009, the Australian market declined by 54 %, compared to the peak to trough decline of 57 % in the US market, 60 % in the Japanese market, and 61 % in the European market (Debelle 2009). At the time of their most recent lows, the Australian stock market had returned to its level seen during mid-2003, the Japanese market was back at levels last seen in 1984, and the US market had fallen back to the levels last seen in the mid-1990s (Debelle 2009).

In order to present the impact of the 2008 global financial crisis, this chapter will first graphically compare the overall economic development of the five countries during the time period from 2005 to 2010. Then, it elaborates on the impact of the financial crisis on each country individually in the sequence of Australia, Canada, Japan, New Zealand, and the USA.

The impact of the 2008 global financial crisis on each country can be easily observed from Figs. 2.1, 2.2, 2.3 and 2.4, which show the percentage of real GDP

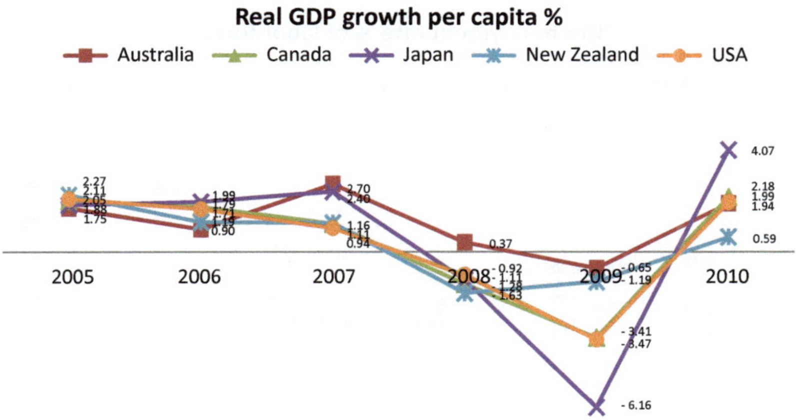


**Fig. 2.1** Real GDP growth per capita of the five advanced countries, 2005–2010

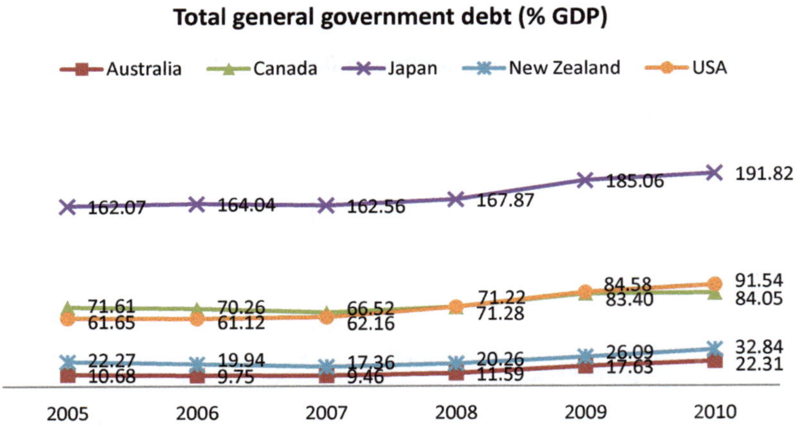


**Fig. 2.2** Total general government debt (percentage of GDP) of the five advanced countries, 2005–2010

growth per capita, total general government debt percentage of GDP, unemployment rate of labor force, and consumer price inflation (CPI).

## Comparisons of the Five Countries

This section presents four figures in order to examine these five advanced countries (Australia, Canada, Japan, New Zealand, and the USA) as a whole from 2005 to 2010. Figure 2.1 shows that all the five countries started to have negative *real GDP*

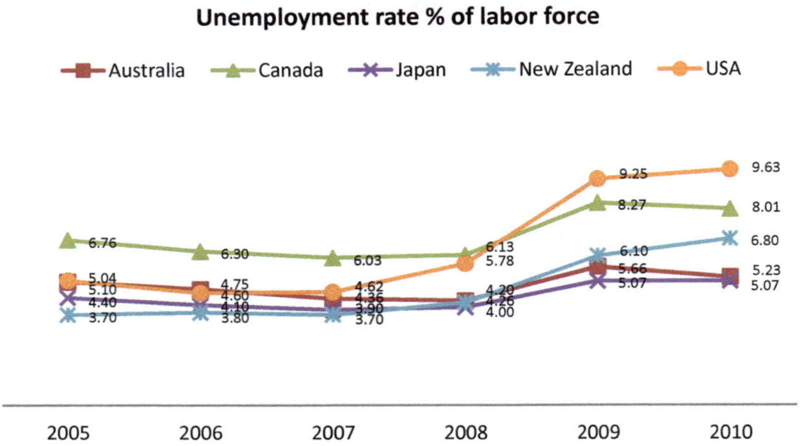


**Fig. 2.3** Percentage of unemployment rate of labor force for the five advanced countries, 2005–2010

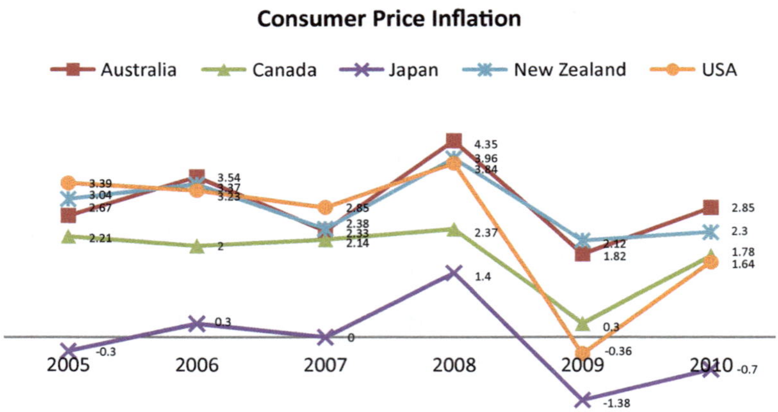


**Fig. 2.4** Consumer Price Inflation of the five advanced countries, 2005–2010

*growth* (except Australia) from 2008, reached their deepest decline in 2009, and then rebounded to a positive growth in 2010. Among them, Australia had the least growth fluctuation, followed by New Zealand. Over the 6 years, the real GDP growth patterns of Canada and the USA are almost identical. Japan had the greatest growth decline of −6.16 % in 2009, yet its upturn in 2010 was also the sharpest (+4.07 %).

In terms of the total *general government debt* as a percentage of the GDP, Fig. 2.2 indicates that government debts of the five countries were relatively stable for the first 3 years (2005–2007). However, their government debt increased continuously from 2008 to 2010, reflecting their increasing financial needs during and after the financial crisis. Overall, there were three debt levels in these five countries: Japan had the highest level, Canada and the USA were in the middle, and Australia and New Zealand had the lowest levels.

Reinhart and Rogoff (2009) reported findings from their research on financial crises over the last 800 years that the aftermath of a financial crisis brings slow and halted growth, sustained high unemployment, and surging public debt—with the overhang of public and private debts being the most crucial impediment to a normal recovery from the recession.

Figure 2.3 shows that the *unemployment* rates of the five countries were relatively stable for the first 4 years (2005–2008), except for the USA. The earlier rising unemployment in the USA in 2008 explains the immediate impact being the epicenter of the financial crisis. Interestingly, its close neighbor Canada was not affected until 2009. All the five countries had a drastic increase in their unemployment rates in 2009, with the USA having the most serious unemployment situation, followed by Canada, New Zealand, Australia, and Japan. In 2010, only New Zealand and the USA had a continuous increase in the unemployment rate. Among the five countries, Australia and Japan had the least unemployment fluctuation over the period of 6 years.

Figure 2.4 shows the CPI of the five countries. Over the period of 6 years, CPI development patterns of these countries were quite similar, except for Canada. Canada's CPI was relatively stable, except for a drastic drop in 2009 that shows the impact of the financial crisis. All the countries had CPI increases in 2008, including the originally deflated Japanese economy. In 2010, most of the countries had resumed their CPI to their precrisis level, except for the USA, which showed a decrease in CPI.

In general, Figs. 2.1, 2.2, 2.3 and 2.4 indicate that the general economy of these five countries was indeed affected by this financial crisis statistically. Overall, their real GDP growth was down in 2008 and 2009 but rebounded in 2010; general government debt gradually increased after 2008; unemployment rate clearly went up in 2009; and the CPI was up in 2008 and then down in 2009.

In what follows, we briefly describe the impact of the 2008 global financial crisis on these five advanced countries. The depth of the report depends on the publicly available data (in English) for each economy. For readers to gain a general picture about the efforts that each country has put in to mitigating the negative impact of the financial crisis, we have summarized the details of the stimulus packages implemented by these countries in Appendix 1. Note that the reported package is based on publicly available data and is not an exhaustive list. In addition, the reported amounts of stimulus packages were based on the exchange rate at the time of each stimulus, and thus may vary. Readers can also refer to Appendix 2 for the important meetings conducted by key global leaders during this financial crisis.

## *Australia*

In recent decades, Australia has transformed itself into an internationally competitive, advanced market economy, focusing on services, technologies, and high-value-added manufactured goods. However, its exports remain heavily concentrated on mining and agriculture (Heritage 2012). Mainly due to the economic reforms adopted in the 1980s, the Australian economy grew for 17 consecutive years before this global financial crisis (CIA 2012).

With the global recession, the Australian economy was also hit hard by this financial crisis. In the last quarter of 2008, businesses ran down their stocks by US$ 2.2 billion (A$ 3.4 billion) (in real terms), which was the largest fall on record. Consumer confidence plummeted along with consumption (Kennedy 2009). In October 2008, the Reserve Bank of Australia Board cut interest rates by 100 basis points. The Australian government also announced that it would make a provision to guarantee all Australian bank deposits and, for a fee, the wholesale funding of Australia's banks. To mitigate the negative impact, the Australian government announced a US$ 7.1 billion (A$ 10.4 billion) stimulus package of around 1 % of its GDP. The package comprised of US$ 5.9 billion (A$ 8.7 billion) that would be provided to 4 million pensioners and low-income families in the form of cash bonuses, US$ 1 billion (A$ 1.5 billion) for housing construction, and US$ 128 million (A$ 187 million) for 56,000 new training places (Access Economics 2008; Kennedy 2009). The stimulus package was designed to rescue the housing and consumption (representing over 60 % of the Australian economy) and to be quick acting with significant cash bonuses paid to those in need within weeks of the announcement (Kennedy 2009). In early December 2008, the Australian government announced large-scale infrastructure projects amounting to US$ 3 billion (A$ 4.7 billion) to prepare for the possibility of a deeper and long-lasting global financial crisis than expected. In late 2008, the depreciating Australian dollar worked as an effective automatic stabilizer (Kennedy 2009).

In early February 2009, the Australian government announced its second stimulus package of US$ 27.2 billion (A$ 42 billion) titled the "Nation Building and Jobs Plan," designed to support up to 90,000 jobs in 2008–2009 and 2009–2010, and to boost the economic growth by about 0.5 and 0.75–1 % of its GDP in 2008–2009 and 2009–2010, respectively (Kennedy 2009; Treasurer 2009). In planning for a fast impact, 70 % of the second stimulus package comprised of infrastructure spending, focusing on quick-starting mid-scale infrastructure. The package included US$ 9.5 billion (A$ 14.7 billion) to be spent on school infrastructure, US$ 4.3 billion (A$ 6.6 billion) on social and defense housing, US$ 2.5 billion (A$ 3.9 billion) on energy efficiency measures (most of which will go to insulating the ceilings of existing homes), and US$ 576 million (A$ 890 million) on road, rail, and small-scale community infrastructure projects (Kennedy 2009). The package also included over US$ 7.8 billion (A$ 12 billion) to fund a range of additional one-off transfer payments targeted at a variety of low- and middle-income groups, with about half the Australian population receiving payments (ILO 2010a). There was also an additional US$ 1.7 billion (A$ 2.7 billion) for private business investment through a business investment tax break (Kennedy 2009). The direct cash payments to low- and middle-income households have had a significant impact on business and consumer confidence, which began recovering strongly in mid-2009 (ILO 2010a).

In addition, the Australian government quickly followed its second stimulus package with a jobs package aimed at younger persons. With the US$ 970 million

(A$ 1.5 billion) package provided by the federal government, the states were required to guarantee a training place to all unemployed people aged 25 years and under. The government anticipated that this package would provide up to 135,000 young Australians with higher qualifications and result in a more skilled workforce in preparation for the return of normal labor market demand. An additional US$ 14.2 billion (A$ 22 billion) budget for large-scale infrastructure was also announced, which helped the Australian government to outline its medium-term fiscal strategy (Kennedy 2009).

Overall, the Australian economy entered the global financial crisis with a strong base. GDP grew by 3.7% in the 2007–2008 financial year (ending June 30), and the unemployment rate stood at 4.2% (ILO 2010a). The government also had a substantial fiscal surplus for the stimulus measures introduced after the onset of the crisis. The country avoided a recession, with only one quarterly decline in GDP, a 0.9% drop in the fourth quarter of 2008. Growth was driven by the government's swiftly introduced and substantial stimulus measures, along with China's robust demand for Australian commodities (ILO 2010a). The government's stimulus took effect mainly for its effective design centered on the following three broad phases: first, one-off cash payments to low- and middle-income groups, which were rapidly disbursed and had an almost immediate impact on the consumption expenditure, retail sales, and the economic growth; second, relatively rapid investments in social infrastructure, including schools, health, and housing; and third, major new investments in economic infrastructure that were more medium term in nature (ILO 2010a).

In general, Australia weathered the world recession better than almost all other advanced economies (Debelle 2009; OECD 2010). Its GDP started to grow in the first quarter of 2009 and consumer confidence rebounded swiftly (Kennedy 2009). The Australian economy grew by 1.2% during 2009—the best performance among the OECD countries (CIA 2012).

## *Canada*

Canada enjoys a substantial trade surplus with the USA, with three-fourths of its exports to the USA each year. Given its great natural resources, skilled labor force, and modern capital plant, Canada enjoyed solid economic growth from 1993 through 2007 (CIA 2012). During this global financial crisis, the Canadian economy dipped into a sharp recession in the final months of 2008 due to its close ties with the USA. Moreover, its strong energy and natural resources suffered as the world economic slowdown brought about lower demand and weaker prices for commodities (Bergevin 2008). As a result, Canada had an annual growth rate that slid markedly to 0.4% in 2008 and posted its first fiscal deficit in 2009 after 12 years of surplus, with the GDP contracted by 2.6% in 2009 compared to the year earlier (ILO 2010b; CIA 2012). The credit crunch and falling commodity prices caused Canada to lose more than 100,000 jobs in the last 2 months of 2008 (BBC 2009). Growth did not return until the third quarter of 2009 and accelerated to 1.2% in the fourth quarter (ILO 2010b).

To help stabilize the economy, the Canadian government announced on October 10, 2008 and November 12, 2008 that it would purchase US$ 21 billion (C$ 25 billion) in insured mortgage pools and would acquire another US$ 40.7 billion (C$ 50 billion) in securities, respectively, to maintain the availability of longer-term credit in Canada (Chossudovsky 2009; Silva 2009). Simultaneously, the government announced that it would "guarantee…more than US$ 162.6 billion (C$ 200 billion) to pay back new loans made to Canadian financial institutions" (Silva 2009).

In March 2009, Canada announced its Economic Action Plan, which totaled US$ 37.8 billion (C$ 47.3 billion) as a federal stimulus (ILO 2012b). The stimulus program comprised of public spending on goods and services, such as building homes and energy efficiency spending, boosting consumer spending through income tax cut and improved access to finance, and protecting jobs and supporting automotive, forestry, and manufacturing industries (ILO 2010b). Green investment comprised 8 % of the stimulus spending and over 13 % of Canada's federal stimulus was directly aimed at labor market initiatives (ILO 2010b). Particularly, Canada's Work-Sharing Program helped the companies and workers to continue working together productively through difficult times (ILO 2010b). The 2009 budget set out spending of US$ 32 billion (C$ 40 billion) over 5 years (BBC 2009).

During the crisis, Canadian banks remained profitable, mainly because they were well capitalized and well positioned to withstand economic shocks (Bergevin 2008; Porter 2010). Canada's banking system has been ranked as the most sound in the world by the World Economic Forum; it did not experience a crisis in 2008 (Schuler 2011). In addition, with the six largest domestic banks holding more than 90 % of banking industry assets, the banking industry is relatively stable.

Although Canadian financial institutions could not avoid the impact of this global financial crisis, none was excessively impacted by toxic assets and, most importantly, they continued to lend (Lynch 2010). Statistics showed that sub-prime loans accounted for less than 5 % of the new mortgages in Canada, compared to 22 % in the USA in 2006. By estimation, more than 75 % of Canadian mortgages were held by financial institutions on their balance sheet in a more traditional fashion with an average asset-to-capital ratio of 18 (Durocher 2008; Bergevin 2008). In addition, the Bank of Canada massively injected liquidities while broadening the range of securities held under resale agreements to help financial markets run smoothly. They also reached swap agreements with other central banks, issued additional Treasury bills, and cut its key interest rates by 50 basis points to support the Canadian economy in a time of crisis (Durocher 2008). These measures have helped Canada withstand the external financial shock fairly well.

## *Japan*

Japan's overall real economic growth was spectacular for three decades—a 10 % average in the 1960s, a 5 % average in the 1970s, and a 4 % average in the 1980s. However, growth slowed down markedly in the 1990s, averaging just 1.7 %, largely because of the aftereffects of inefficient investments and an asset price bubble (CIA 2012).

The Japanese financial sector was not heavily exposed to sub-prime mortgages or their derivative instruments; thus, the country weathered the initial effect of the recent global credit crunch fairly well. However, a sharp downturn in business investment and global demand for Japan's exports in late 2008 hit its export-dependent economy hard, especially since the USA accounted for 20.1 % of Japan's exports in 2007 (Nanto 2009). Furthermore, Japan holds US$ 74.5 billion in debt issued by Fannie Mae and Freddie Mac, two of the largest housing loan providers in the USA. In addition, claims by the Japanese banks and security firms against the Lehman Brothers totaled in billions of dollars (Hays 2009).

As a result, Japan's trade deficit touched US$ 2.3 billion (¥ 223 billion) in November 2008 and reached a record of US$ 10.6 billion (¥ 952.6 billion) in January 2009 (Hays 2011). Its GDP declined 12.1 % in the fourth quarter in 2008 and crashed 14.2 % in the first quarter of 2009, which was the steepest fall on record (Hays 2011). The Nikkei stood at 15,307 at the end of 2007 and fell to 6,448 in 2008, a fall of 42.1 %, the largest ever percentage fall in a single year, worse than the Dow Jones (−36 %) and the London FTSE (−33.1 %) (Hays 2011). The main cause of the dramatic drop was the exodus of foreign investment, which had accounted for 60 % of the trading volume on Japan's stock market in the recent years (Hays 2011).

Exports plunged almost 50 % in February 2009 as demand for Japanese cars and electronics dropped; this was the biggest decline since the government began keeping such records (Hays 2011). Business and consumer confidence reached its lowest level in 34 years. The Bank of Japan injected trillions of Japanese yen into the money market and offered US$ 10.9 billion (¥ 1 trillion) in loans to encourage banks to lend money and purchase government bonds to make money available for investments (Hays 2011).

The Japanese government launched stimulus packages to the total of US$ 568 billion, amounting to 5 % of its GDP (which is about the same size as the USA and above the average of 3.9 % for OECD countries). The packages particularly emphasized on sustaining credit flows and stabilizing markets, encouraging lending to small and medium-sized enterprises (SMEs), stabilizing the stock market, providing emergency loans to firms, facilitating corporate financing, and lowering the policy interest rate from 0.5 to 0.1 % by the end of 2008 (Hays 2011; OECD 2009). In addition, public works projects, tax cuts, programs to address global warming, and health and childcare are also on the agenda. Specifically, the package supports a subsidy of US$ 2,718 (¥ 250,000) for people who replaced gas-guzzling vehicles with fuel-efficient ones, US$ 10.9 billion (¥ 1 trillion) in housing subsidies and other support for temporary workers who had been discharged from their accommodation, and US$ 130.5 billion (¥ 12 trillion) in loans and grants to banks. In addition, more than US$ 21.7 billion (¥ 2 trillion) was given out to citizens to stimulate spending with US$ 130 (¥ 12,000) in coupons to each Japanese resident and an additional US$ 87 (¥ 8,000) to those under the age of 18 and over the age of 65 (Hays 2011). The package was projected to raise real growth by 2 % and create around

400,000 to 500,000 jobs (Hays 2011). The International Labor Office (2010c) has provided details of the Japanese stimulus package, summarized in Appendix 1.

Despite the drastic economic downturn, Japan was one of the first countries to recover, with positive growth figures at the end of 2009 (Hays 2011). In mid-June 2009, the Nikkei rose above 10,000 and the economy grew by 3.7 % in the second quarter of 2009 (Hays 2011). GDP increased by 4.8 and 4.6 % in the third and fourth quarter of 2009, respectively. The trade surplus rose for 6 months in a row with a robust demand from China, which was seen as an indicator that the recession was ending and that recovery was real. In late November 2009, the yen rose to its highest value against the dollar in 14 years (Hays 2011).

To boost the economy further, in December 2009 the Japanese government announced another US$ 80 million (¥ 7.2 billion) stimulus that included funding to local governments to make up for reduced taxes, support to the financial sector, subsidies to the environmental sector to continue the eco-points program, and money to homeowners for energy-savings measures (Hays 2011).

Overall, the Japanese economy began to contract in the second quarter of 2008, with continued steep declines through the first quarter of 2009; however, a small growth of an average 0.8 % returned in the second quarter of 2009 (ILO 2010c). Unemployment rates rose to a high of 5.7 % in August 2009 (CIA 2012). Despite some growth at the end of the year, the Japanese economy shrunk by 5.4 % in 2009 (Hays 2011). Clearly, the government stimulus spending helped the Japanese economy recover in late 2009, however with a government budget deficit of around 10 % in 2010 (OECD 2009).

## *New Zealand*

Over the past 20 years, New Zealand has been transformed from an agrarian economy, dependent on concessionary British market access, to a more industrialized, free market economy that can compete globally (CIA 2012). Per capita income adjusted by purchasing power parity rose for 10 consecutive years until 2007.

In the first half of the 2000s, New Zealand's debt-driven consumer spending drove robust growth with a large balance of payments deficit. As a result, its economy fell into recession before the start of the global financial crisis (CIA 2012). The balance of the non-financial private sector deteriorated markedly as the increase in property prices and perceived wealth prompted additional household spending. The widening of the current account deficit was largely financed by bank-intermediated foreign credit, adding to the already high external debt (OECD 2011d). In addition, weak business investment and low national saving have contributed to poor growth performance (OECD 2011d).

The New Zealand economy contracted throughout 2008 and early 2009. The initial triggers of recession in early 2008 were domestic factors, including drought and tight monetary policy to combat growing inflation pressures. This domestic-led recession was escalated by the global financial crisis in mid-September 2008 (Treasury 2009). Following the intensification of the global financial crisis, the New

Zealand economy deteriorated sharply. Business and consumer confidence plummeted as uncertainty dominated the global financial and economic environment. External demand decreased and inbound tourism continued to weaken. Economic activity contracted by 0.9 % in the last quarter of 2008, especially in manufacturing, construction, wholesale, and retail trade (Treasury 2010).

To alleviate the negative impacts, the New Zealand Reserve Bank introduced a range of facilities to ensure that adequate liquidity was available to the banking sector for restoring confidence and providing banks with improved access to wholesale funding (Treasury 2010). The New Zealand government launched personal income tax cuts on October 1, 2008 and introduced further tax reductions effective from April 1, 2009 (Treasury 2010). Other measures include an accelerated package of *ready-to-roll* infrastructure projects covering the housing, transport, education, and energy sectors at an estimated cost of almost US$ 281.6 million (NZ$ 500 million) and a temporary relief package designed to assist small and medium-sized businesses that make up the largest proportion of New Zealand businesses (Treasury 2010).

As global uncertainty intensified in the second quarter of 2009, the New Zealand economy fell a further 0.8 % from the previous quarter and private consumption fell 1.2 %—the largest quarterly decline since 1991 (Treasury 2010). However, its manufacturing and export sectors were less affected by the global financial crisis than many other countries, partly because of its commodity exports, such as dairy products, which remained in demand. In addition, its main market for manufactured exports, Australia, was also less affected by this global financial crisis. Furthermore, the banking sector in New Zealand is predominantly foreign-owned (96.1 % in December 2008), especially by the Australians (Tripe 2009). Fortunately, the Australian banking system was one of the strongest internationally during this financial crisis (Tripe 2009), which safeguarded New Zealand's banks from being ravaged by the crisis.

In March 2009, net permanent and long-term migration increased sharply, with arrivals remaining strong while departures plummeted as job prospects offshore continued to deteriorate. The combination of exceptionally low fixed mortgage interest rates and rapidly increasing net migration led to house prices increasing in the second quarter of 2009, after having declined 9.8 % from the December 2007 peak (Treasury 2010). Renewed optimism in the global economic environment resulted in a sharp increase in business confidence, leading to a modest positive growth of 0.2 % in the second quarter of 2009, thus marking the end of a five-quarter recession (Treasury 2010).

During this financial crisis, New Zealand was ranked the seventh least affected out of the 30 OECD member nations (Treasury 2010). With gradual recovery, its current account deficit fell from 8.9 % of its GDP in September 2008 to 3.1 % in September 2009. However, the unemployment rate rose from a record-low of 3.5 % in late 2007 to 7.3 % in December 2009 (Treasury 2010) and the economy posted a 1.7 % decline in 2009 (CIA 2012). Net debt fell to 6 % of its GDP in 2007–2008 but rose to 9.5 % of the GDP in 2008–2009, as a result of additional borrowing undertaken to offset the government's operating deficit (Treasury 2010). In general, New Zealand's economic performance was supported by a sound financial system, growth in key trading partners—China and Australia—strong commodity exports, falling emigration, and monetary and fiscal stimulus (Treasury 2009). These factors also helped pull New Zealand out of the recession in the second quarter of 2009.

## *The United States*

The US economy is the world's largest, with services accounting for more than 70% of its economic activity. However, the USA remains the world's largest producer of manufactured goods (Heritage 2012). For decades, the US firms enjoyed greater flexibility than their counterparts in Western Europe and Japan did, with respect to making decisions to expand capital plants, to lay off surplus workers, and to develop new products (CIA 2012). In the early 1990s, the US government pursued an expansionary fiscal policy, which led to a budget deficit of 3.1% of its GDP in 2008; such deficit was unsustainable, given the growth of entitlement spending in health care and retirement, and the increasing retiring baby-boomer cohort (Falke 2010).

This financial crisis originated from the US housing sector with substantial mortgage debts by households. Mortgage originators took the risk of extending loans to borrowers that were previously not considered creditworthy, which led to an accumulation of low-quality sub-prime debts (Michelis 2009). In addition, the mortgage originators used a securitization process to sell mortgage loans and used the money to make more loans. In other words, the securitization turned illiquid assets of individual mortgage loans into marketable securities that could be bought, sold, and traded on secondary markets. At the end of 2006, the total outstanding mortgage-backed securities (MBSs) were nearly US$ 6.5 trillion in the USA, compared to US$ 400 billion in the Euro area and less than 20% of securitized residential mortgages in the United Kingdom (Michelis 2009). After the mortgage market collapsed, various financial institutions were seriously affected, including mortgage lenders, commercial as well as investment banks, and the two major government-sponsored enterprises—Fannie Mae and Freddie Mac.

The financial crisis that emerged in mid-2007 caused considerable economic disruptions in the USA and elsewhere. In the USA, the economic recession actually began in December 2007 (ILO 2010d) and then burst into a financial crisis after the collapse of the Lehman Brothers in September 2008. The global economic downturn, the sub-prime mortgage crisis, investment bank failures, falling home prices, and tight credit pushed the USA into a recession by mid-2008 (CIA 2012). To help stabilize financial markets, the US Congress established a US$ 700 billion Troubled Asset Relief Program (TARP) in October 2008 to rescue certain banks and financial institutions. Citigroup, for example, received US$ 45 billion, Bank of America US$ 25 billion, and AIG US$ 180 billion (Los Angeles Times 2011). These loans came with certain restrictions, particularly pertaining to executive compensation. On February 17, 2009, the USA signed into law the American Recovery and Reinvestment Act (ARRA)—a US$ 787 billion bill, which was about 5.8% of its GDP, to stimulate the economy (ILO 2010d). The money was to be used over 10 years, with two-thirds on additional spending and one-third on tax cuts, in order to create jobs and to help the economy recover (CIA 2012).

The stimulus package included roughly US$ 300 billion in tax breaks for individuals and businesses; more than US$ 250 billion in direct aid to states and individuals; and almost US$ 200 billion to modernize and to improve infrastructure, with "green" investments comprising about 12% of the total stimulus spending (ILO 2010d). As of September 30, 2009, US$ 173 billion of the US$ 787 billion had been paid out by the federal government. The Recovery Act allocated US$ 82.5 billion to strengthen social protection and to improve employment prospects through labor market programs. A number of these programs have been quite effective, particularly the unemployment insurance program; Supplemental Nutrition Assistance Program (SNAP, formerly Food Stamps); Consolidated Omnibus Budget Reconciliation Act (COBRA, which continues to provide access to health insurance for the unemployed); training grants for green jobs and emerging industry sectors; and work-sharing programs (ILO 2010d). Readers can refer to Appendix 1 for the details of the US stimulus packages.

With the stimulus programs and bank bailouts, the US national debt jumped from 40% of its GDP in 2008 to nearly 70% a year later (Falke 2010). By the end of 2009, the trade deficit reached an unprecedented figure of US$ 821 billion, and the current account deficit reached US$ 731 billion, about 5% of its GDP (Falke 2010). Growth, production, employment, and trade have all been hit. In the USA, growth contracted by 6.2% in the fourth quarter of 2008, the worst such fall since 1982; unemployment rose to 7.6% in January 2009, and reached 10% by September 2009 (Falke 2010).

The US government and the Federal Reserve (Fed) were swift and resolute in their response to mitigate the financial shock. By December 2008, the Fed had reduced the federal funds rate significantly from 5.25% in 2007 to a target range of 0–0.25% (Falke 2010). In addition, the Fed used several new facilities to lend directly to financial institutions, leading to outstanding loans of more than US$ 3 trillion. The Fed has also bought commercial assets worth about US$ 800 billion, including mortgage-backed securities (Falke 2010). Social protection accounted for a large proportion of the ARRA, amounting to roughly US$ 80 billion. Health and education policies have also fared well under the ARRA, with US$ 14.2 billion earmarked for health-care programs and US$ 106 billion for education. An additional US$ 4 billion have been allocated for pre-school education (Falke 2010). In order to support purchasing power, the government's most significant measure has been the US$ 106 billion Making Work Pay tax credit, followed by the child tax credit of US$ 14.8 billion.

With these efforts, in the third quarter of 2009, there was a 2.8% positive growth uptick with the trend continuing in the fourth quarter at a rate of 5.7% (ILO 2010d). However, consumer confidence remained at very weak levels, house prices and construction activities stabilized, and business confidence indicators were positive again (Falke 2010).

The impact of the financial crisis on the labor market was very pronounced. In the wake of the economic recession, the unemployment rate grew steeply, reaching a peak of 10.1% in October 2009, the highest rate since 1983. During the financial crisis, a total of 8.4 million jobs were lost in the USA (ILO 2010d).

# Chapter 3
# National Intellectual Capital Development of the Five Advanced Countries

## National Intellectual Capital Development

The NIC measurement model in this study is based upon the indicators described in Appendix 3, containing human capital, market capital, process capital, renewal capital, and financial capital. This model has been statistically proven for its validity and reliability. The definitions of the indicators are listed in Appendix 4. This booklet series covers a total of 48 countries in 11 country clusters (see Appendix 5 for details).

For a full picture of all the 48 countries, refer to Appendix 6 that exhibits the scores and rankings of human capital, market capital, process capital, renewal capital, financial capital, and overall NIC covered in this booklet series. Table 3.1 summarizes the status of these five countries compared with the 48 countries reported in Appendix 6. Appendix 7 provides the individual economic profiles with additional statistics. Regarding NIC rankings, the USA ranks at #7, followed by Canada at #12, Australia at #13, Japan at #15, and New Zealand at #21.

From Table 3.1, Australia excels in process capital (#9); Canada performs well in human capital (#6); Japan is relatively good in renewal capital (#7); and the USA has high financial capital (#3) and renewal capital (#5).

Figures 3.1, 3.2, 3.3, 3.4, 3.5, and 3.6 compare human capital, market capital, process capital, renewal capital, financial capital, and NIC for the five countries. All individual capital scores are based on a 1–10 scale, with the NIC score being the sum of the five capital scores.

### *Human Capital*

National human capital represents a nation's investment in nurturing qualified human resources, such as higher education enrollment, skilled labor, and public expenditure in education. Human capital is a long-term-oriented NIC (Lin and Edvinsson 2011, p. 323), which takes time to develop and is not susceptible to external impact. Figure 3.1 shows that the human capital of these five countries remained

C. Y.-Y. Lin et al., *National Intellectual Capital and the Financial Crisis in Australia, Canada, Japan, New Zealand, and the United States*, SpringerBriefs in Economics, DOI 10.1007/978-1-4614-9308-2_3, © The Author(s) 2014

**Table 3.1** National intellectual capital scores and ranking of the five advanced countries spanning 2005–2010

| | Human capital | | Market capital | | Process capital | | Renewal capital | | Financial capital | | NIC | |
|---|---|---|---|---|---|---|---|---|---|---|---|---|
| Country | Score | Ranking | Score | Ranking | Score | Ranking | Score | Ranking | Score | Ranking | Score | Ranking |
| Australia | 7.205 | 15 | 6.199 | 12 | 6.938 | 9 | 4.927 | 16 | 9.695 | 11 | 34.964 | 13 |
| Canada | 7.855 | 6 | 6.137 | 13 | 6.464 | 15 | 5.064 | 14 | 9.710 | 9 | 35.229 | 12 |
| Japan | 7.581 | 10 | 4.820 | 34 | 6.209 | 18 | 6.473 | 7 | 9.576 | 19 | 34.659 | 15 |
| New Zealand | 7.123 | 18 | 5.999 | 15 | 6.460 | 16 | 3.701 | 22 | 9.380 | 26 | 32.662 | 21 |
| USA | 7.695 | 7 | 5.348 | 25 | 6.558 | 13 | 6.715 | 5 | 9.886 | 3 | 36.202 | 7 |

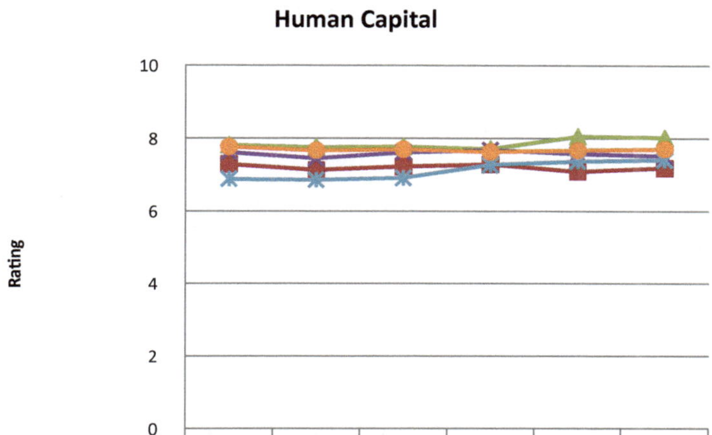


| | 2005 | 2006 | 2007 | 2008 | 2009 | 2010 |
|---|---|---|---|---|---|---|
| Australia | 7.29 | 7.13 | 7.23 | 7.29 | 7.09 | 7.19 |
| Canada | 7.81 | 7.76 | 7.77 | 7.71 | 8.06 | 8.02 |
| Japan | 7.62 | 7.46 | 7.62 | 7.69 | 7.58 | 7.52 |
| New Zealand | 6.88 | 6.86 | 6.92 | 7.28 | 7.38 | 7.42 |
| USA | 7.77 | 7.67 | 7.70 | 7.64 | 7.68 | 7.71 |

**Fig. 3.1** Human capital of Australia, Canada, Japan, New Zealand, and the USA

relatively stable over the 6 years, with Canada and New Zealand having a little increase in 2009 and 2010.

## *Market Capital*

National market capital represents international trade and relationships such as cross-border ventures, globalization, and exports of goods. Figure 3.2 shows three levels of market capital, with Australia, Canada, and New Zealand overlapping with each other at the high level. The market capital of these three countries decreased in 2008, yet rebounded in 2010. The market capital for the USA is in the middle level, with a clear decrease in 2008; yet it rebounded in 2009 and 2010. Market capital for Japan is in the low level, also with a decrease in 2008. Unlike the USA, Japan did not have a clear rebound after the financial crisis; instead, its market capital slid particularly in 2010.

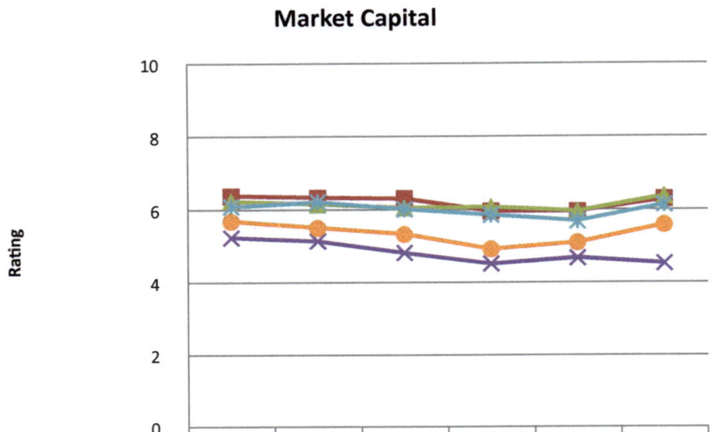


| | 2005 | 2006 | 2007 | 2008 | 2009 | 2010 |
|---|---|---|---|---|---|---|
| Australia | 6.37 | 6.32 | 6.31 | 5.95 | 5.95 | 6.29 |
| Canada | 6.24 | 6.14 | 6.05 | 6.07 | 5.95 | 6.37 |
| Japan | 5.24 | 5.15 | 4.82 | 4.52 | 4.67 | 4.53 |
| New Zealand | 6.09 | 6.22 | 6.02 | 5.85 | 5.68 | 6.14 |
| USA | 5.68 | 5.50 | 5.32 | 4.91 | 5.09 | 5.58 |

**Fig. 3.2** Market capital of Australia, Canada, Japan, New Zealand, and the USA

## *Process Capital*

National process capital represents the infrastructure required for building a prosperous society, such as capital availability, mobile phone subscribers, and government efficiency. Figure 3.3 indicates that the process capital scores of the five countries are not too far from each other and were relatively stable over the 6 years. Nevertheless, Australia and the USA had more noticeable ups and downs. The former experienced a process capital decline in 2009 and the latter an early decline in 2008; however, both rebounded well in 2010. The other three countries did not have too much process capital change, with Japan consistently having the lowest score.

## *Renewal Capital*

National renewal capital represents the capability of research and development (R&D) and innovation, such as R&D spending, scientific articles, and patents. Figure 3.4 shows three renewal capital clusters. Japan and the USA are the countries in the high-level cluster, Australia and Canada in the middle-level cluster, and New

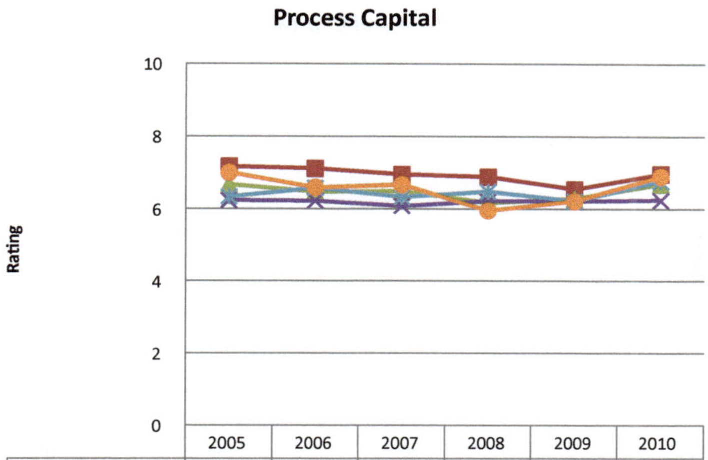


| | 2005 | 2006 | 2007 | 2008 | 2009 | 2010 |
|---|---|---|---|---|---|---|
| Australia | 7.17 | 7.11 | 6.95 | 6.89 | 6.55 | 6.97 |
| Canada | 6.68 | 6.47 | 6.48 | 6.18 | 6.28 | 6.69 |
| Japan | 6.24 | 6.23 | 6.09 | 6.22 | 6.22 | 6.25 |
| New Zealand | 6.35 | 6.59 | 6.33 | 6.49 | 6.23 | 6.78 |
| USA | 7.00 | 6.59 | 6.67 | 5.96 | 6.22 | 6.90 |

**Fig. 3.3** Process capital of Australia, Canada, Japan, New Zealand, and the USA

Zealand by itself consistently in the lowest level. More noticeable changes include that Australia had a renewal capital drop in 2007 and was surpassed by Canada ever since. Japan had a renewal capital increase in 2010, New Zealand had continuous renewal capital decline in 2009 and 2010, and the USA had a renewal capital decline in 2006 and in 2008, however with good rebound in 2009.

## *Financial Capital*

Financial capital is representative of GDP per capita (ppp) in US dollars transformed to a score on a scale of 1–10. The process of score transformation is explained in Appendix 3. Figure 3.5 shows that the five countries do not have too much financial capital difference. However, New Zealand consistently had the lowest and the USA the highest score. In real dollars, the average GDP per capita (ppp) of 2005–2010 was US$37,204 for Australia, US$37,770 for Canada, US$32,655 for Japan, US$26,387 for New Zealand, and US$45,742 for the USA.

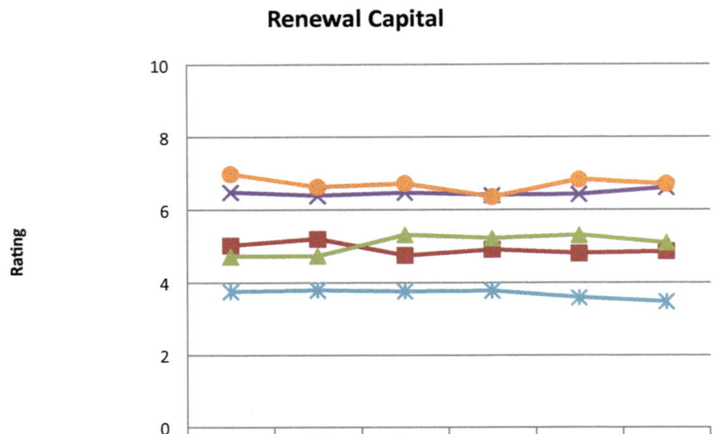


| | 2005 | 2006 | 2007 | 2008 | 2009 | 2010 |
|---|---|---|---|---|---|---|
| Australia | 5.03 | 5.20 | 4.75 | 4.91 | 4.80 | 4.87 |
| Canada | 4.72 | 4.73 | 5.32 | 5.22 | 5.30 | 5.10 |
| Japan | 6.49 | 6.39 | 6.49 | 6.41 | 6.43 | 6.62 |
| New Zealand | 3.76 | 3.80 | 3.77 | 3.79 | 3.59 | 3.49 |
| USA | 6.99 | 6.64 | 6.73 | 6.36 | 6.84 | 6.72 |

**Fig. 3.4** Renewal capital of Australia, Canada, Japan, New Zealand, and the USA

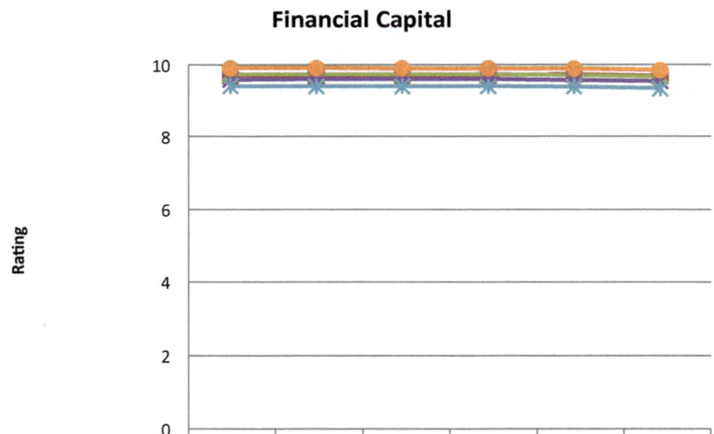


| | 2005 | 2006 | 2007 | 2008 | 2009 | 2010 |
|---|---|---|---|---|---|---|
| Australia | 9.69 | 9.68 | 9.69 | 9.70 | 9.73 | 9.68 |
| Canada | 9.72 | 9.72 | 9.72 | 9.72 | 9.71 | 9.66 |
| Japan | 9.58 | 9.59 | 9.60 | 9.59 | 9.56 | 9.53 |
| New Zealand | 9.40 | 9.39 | 9.39 | 9.39 | 9.38 | 9.32 |
| USA | 9.90 | 9.90 | 9.90 | 9.89 | 9.89 | 9.84 |

**Fig. 3.5** Financial capital of Australia, Canada, Japan, New Zealand, and the USA

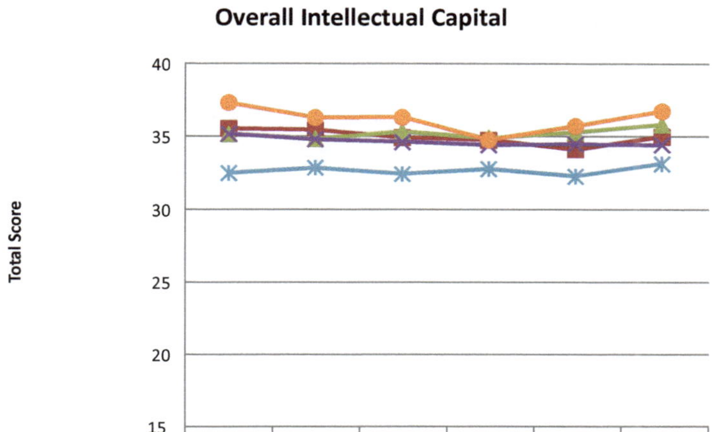


| | 2005 | 2006 | 2007 | 2008 | 2009 | 2010 |
|---|---|---|---|---|---|---|
| Australia | 35.55 | 35.45 | 34.92 | 34.75 | 34.12 | 34.99 |
| Canada | 35.17 | 34.83 | 35.35 | 34.90 | 35.29 | 35.84 |
| Japan | 35.18 | 34.82 | 34.62 | 34.42 | 34.46 | 34.45 |
| New Zealand | 32.48 | 32.86 | 32.43 | 32.79 | 32.27 | 33.14 |
| USA | 37.34 | 36.30 | 36.32 | 34.77 | 35.72 | 36.76 |

**Fig. 3.6** NIC of Australia, Canada, Japan, New Zealand, and the USA

## *National Intellectual Capital*

NIC refers to the overall national intellectual capital comprising the five types of capital described in the sections above. Figure 3.6 presents the trends of overall NIC over the 6 years. In general, the NIC of these countries was relatively stable from 2005 to 2008, except for the USA, which had a clear declining trend up to 2008. Australia had a more noticeable NIC decline from 2008 to 2009, followed by New Zealand. From 2009 to 2010, all the countries had an NIC increase, except for Japan, which had a minute decrease from 34.46 to 34.45. When comparing the NIC scores for 2005 and 2010, Australia, Japan, and the USA had a decrease, whereas Canada and New Zealand had an increase. The NIC development pattern of Fig. 3.6 somewhat explains the economic statuses of these five countries before and after the 2008 global financial crisis. Briefly speaking, from 2005 to 2007, their economic situations were relatively stable, except for the USA which showed signs of decline. The NIC drop for the USA in 2008 depicted its financial troubles. The rebound in 2009 and 2010 explained the recoveries of these five countries.

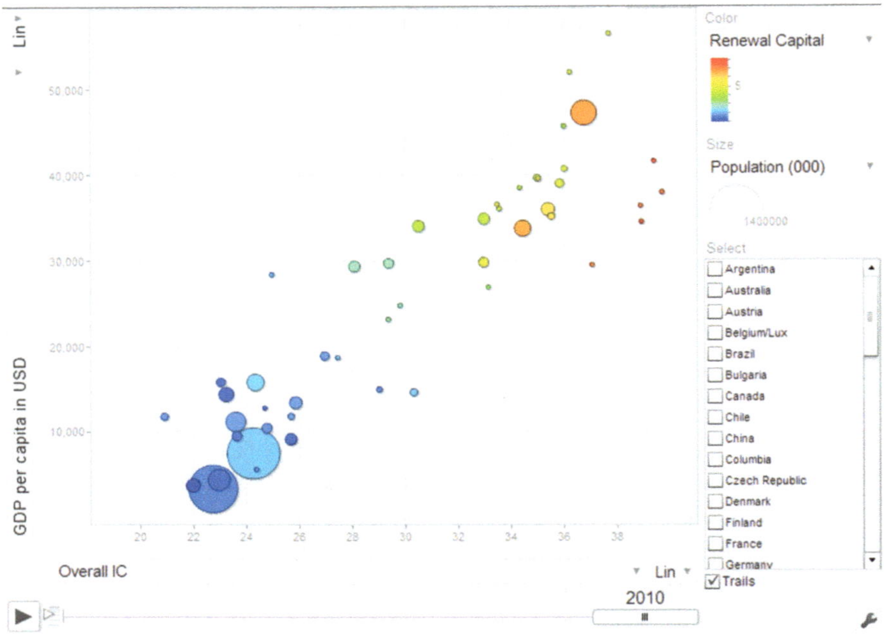


**Fig. 3.7** NIC versus GDP per capita (ppp) for 48 countries in 2010

## The Relationship Between Each Individual Capital and GDP Per Capita (ppp)

We investigate the relationship between each individual capital and economic growth by using Figs. 3.7, 3.8, 3.9, 3.10, 3.11 and 3.12. The graphs have four dimensions: the *X*-axis changes from graph to graph (NIC, human capital, market capital, process capital, and renewal capital), the *Y*-axis is a fixed dimension of GDP per capita (ppp) in US dollars (hereafter termed GDP), the color shade represents renewal capital with red denoting higher levels of renewal capital, and the bubble size denotes the population of a country. Figure 3.7 is the relationship between NIC and GDP for all 48 countries. Figures 3.8–3.12 display the codevelopment of the intellectual capital–GDP relationship over the 6-year timeframe for the five countries. As financial capital is the transformed 1–10 score from GDP, there is no need to plot its relationship against itself. In the figures, 2005 is the starting point tagged with the name of the country, and the end point is 2010.

In particular, Fig. 3.7 is plotted to clearly show a full picture of the relationship between NIC and GDP for 48 countries in the year 2010. The strong positive correlation indicates that the higher the NIC the higher the GDP, and vice versa. Consequently, enhancing NIC is definitely a strategic issue that deserves the attention of national policy makers.

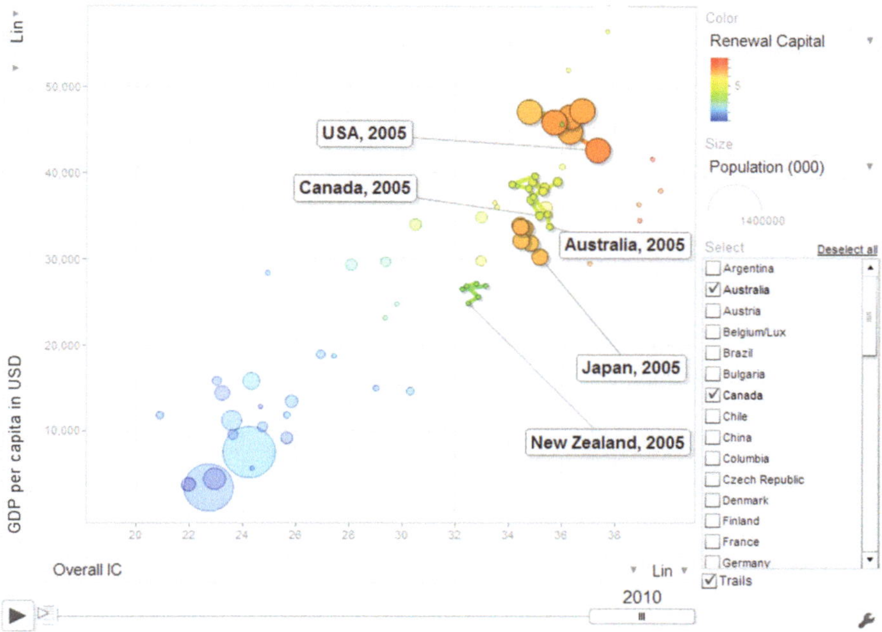


**Fig. 3.8** The development of NIC and GDP per capita (ppp) for Australia, Canada, Japan, New Zealand, and the USA, 2005–2010

With the data of all 48 countries, Fig. 3.8 shows the formation of the NIC and GDP codevelopment continuum from the bottom left to the upper right. The paths of these countries are located at the upper end of the continuum, except that of New Zealand, which is in the middle part. The paths of Australia and Canada are intertwined with each other. Among these five countries, the USA is the leader in terms of NIC and GDP, which agrees with its #5 Global Competitiveness Index (GCI) ranking in 2011–2012 (Fig. 1.1). Its NIC decline is also in concert with its GCI decrease from #2 in 2005–2006 to #5 in 2011–2012. However, Japan has a different scenario. Japan's GCI advanced from #12 in 2005–2006 to #9 in 2011–2012; yet its NIC declined. Japan's NIC–GDP codevelopment path is lower than that of Australia and Canada, even though its GCI is ahead of the two countries in the most recent year. The comparison provides an interesting point of further pursuit concerning the relationship between the intangible NIC and global competitiveness.

Figure 3.9 shows the "human capital–GDP" continuum formation for the 48 countries and the codevelopment paths of the five countries. Again, the development paths of these countries are located at the upper end of the continuum, except for New Zealand, which is in the middle. The relatively vertical path progression of Australia, Japan, and the USA indicates that these three countries had better GDP growth than human capital increase over the 6 years. Canada and New Zealand had good human capital increase with noticeable horizontal progression. Particularly,

**Fig. 3.9** The development of human capital and GDP per capita (ppp) for Australia, Canada, Japan, New Zealand, and the USA, 2005–2010

Canada's GDP grew (vertical progression) until 2008 and New Zealand's GDP stagnated after 2008.

The "market capital-GDP" formation of Fig. 3.10 shows that there is no clear continuum like the one depicted in the last two figures because the data points spread further apart, which means that the correlation between market capital and GDP is not high for the 48 countries as a whole. It also shows that the market capital of advanced countries is not necessarily better than that of developing countries. For example, the market capital of Japan is lower than that of China and India (the two big bubbles at the bottom center of the graph). This figure shows that the USA had the highest GDP, yet its market capital lagged behind that of Australia, Canada, and New Zealand. In addition, Japan is the only country that did not have good market capital rebound after the financial crisis.

Figure 3.11 shows that the belt-shaped continuum reappears. Four of the process capital–GDP codevelopment paths are located at the upper end of the continuum and that of New Zealand is in the middle. For process capital in 2010, Australia did not return to its 2005 level, yet Canada and Japan remained at their 2005 levels, New Zealand had a clear increase, and the USA had a little decrease compared to its 2005 level. The figure also shows that the process capital of Australia was better than that of Canada, and New Zealand was better than that of Japan in 2010.

**Fig. 3.10** The development of market capital and GDP per capita (ppp) for Australia, Canada, Japan, New Zealand, and the USA, 2005–2010

Figure 3.12 shows that there is no clear continuum for the 48 countries. The renewal capital–GDP codevelopment path of the five countries is very different from that of the previous figures. They are spread out in different parts of the graph, yet Australia and Canada are close to each other. The USA continues to be the leader, high in both renewal capital and GDP. If the graph is split into two parts with a dotted line, the paths of Australia, Canada, and New Zealand are tilted toward GDP, which means that comparatively their GDP grows faster than their renewal capital. On the contrary, Japan's path is tilted toward renewal capital. That is, Japan's renewal capital advanced more than its GDP growth.

## Long-Term and Short-Term NIC

In addition to Figs. 3.7–3.12 that show the relationship of each individual capital with GDP, Figs. 3.13, 3.14, 3.15, and 3.16 further plot the relationships between human capital and renewal capital, as well as between market capital and process capital. In our first study (Lin and Edvinsson 2011, p. 324), we found that the combined increase in human capital and renewal capital would lead to a nation's long-term development, whereas the combined increase in market capital and process

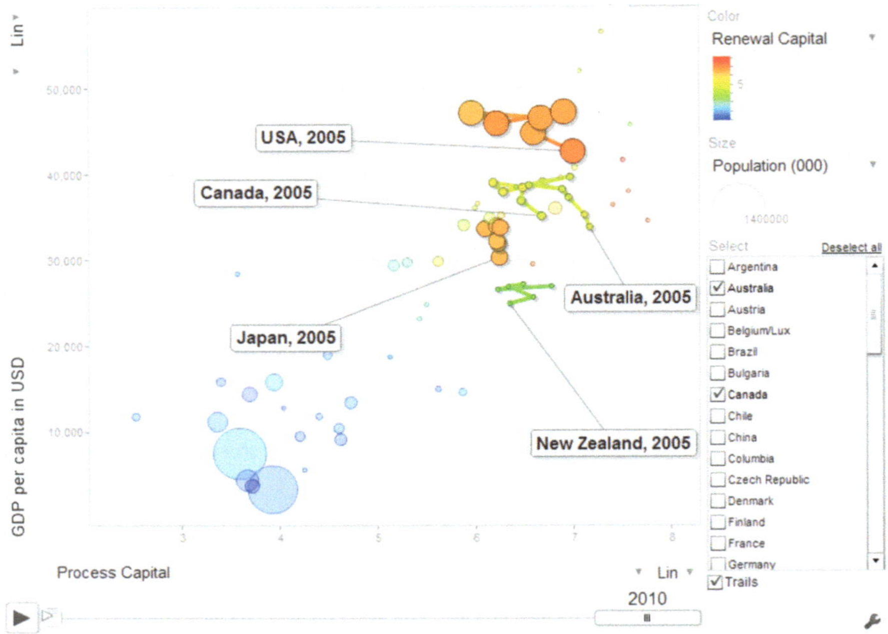


**Fig. 3.11** The development of process capital and GDP per capita (ppp) for Australia, Canada, Japan, New Zealand, and the USA, 2005–2010

capital might result in more immediate economic development. To present their relationships, Figs. 3.13–3.16 map the four capitals on a coordinate with two types of presentation. Based on the same data, Figs. 3.13 and 3.15 exhibit a scatterplot for the five countries only, whereas Figs. 3.14 and 3.16 show all 48 countries in the background so that readers will know the relative positions of these five countries. It is to be noted that the connotation of color shade for Figs. 3.14 and 3.16 has been changed from renewal capital to GDP per capita (ppp).

Both Figs. 3.13 and 3.14 indicate that the long-term NIC of Japan and the USA is at a similar high level, with the USA being a little ahead of Japan. Australia and Canada have similar level of renewal capital, with Canada having better human capital. New Zealand has comparatively a lower long-term NIC than the other four countries; however, its human capital showed good improvement over the years. These two capitals take time to develop and achieve, as human capital is based on unpredictable human performance and renewal capital is the end result of good human capital. Therefore, their development should be planned as early as possible.

Figures 3.15 and 3.16 map market capital and process capital of the five countries on the same coordinate plane. Market capital refers to the general assets embodied in a nation's relationship with international markets, while process capital refers to the national infrastructure, such as information systems and the number of days required to start a new business. In the short term, these are the two types of

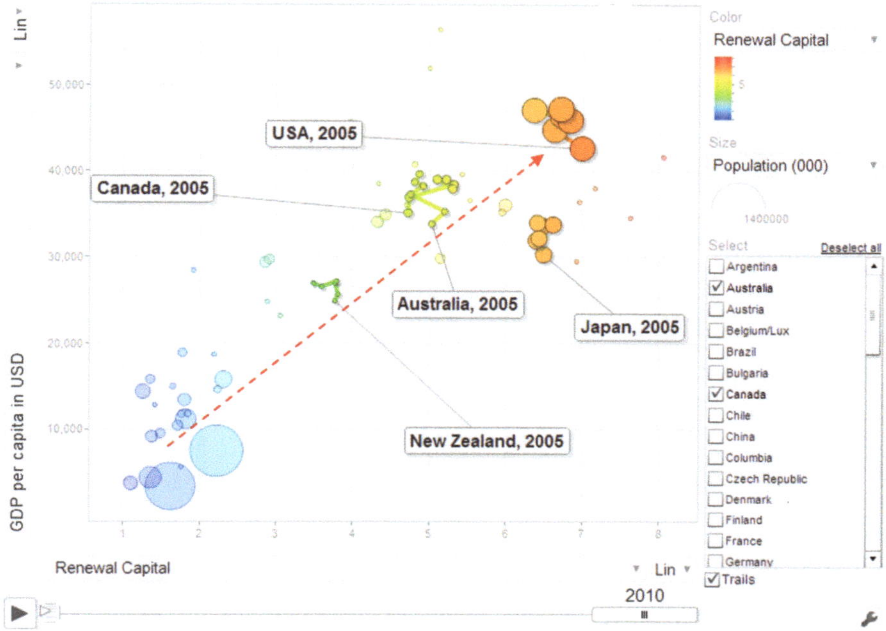


Fig. 3.12 The development of renewal capital and GDP per capita (ppp) for Australia, Canada, Japan, New Zealand, and the USA, 2005–2010

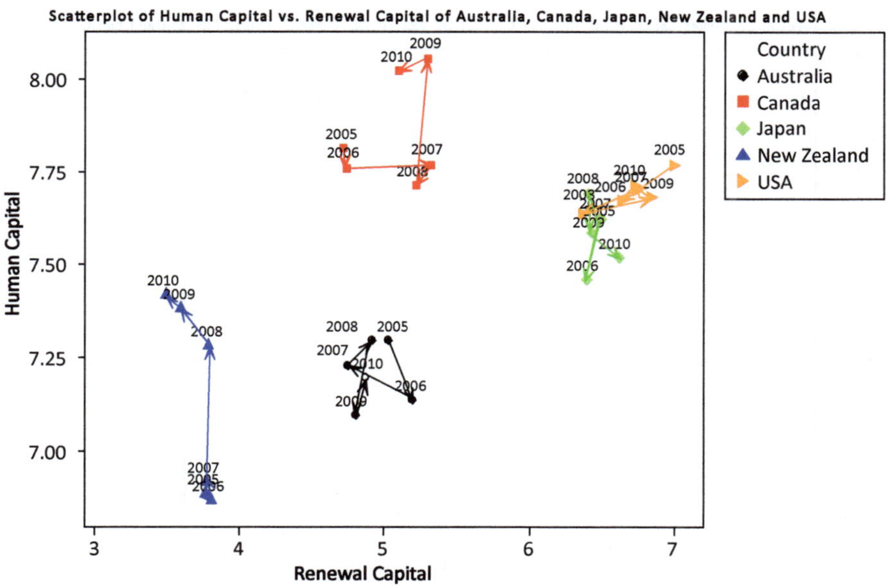


Fig. 3.13 A scatterplot of human capital versus renewal capital for Australia, Canada, Japan, New Zealand, and the USA

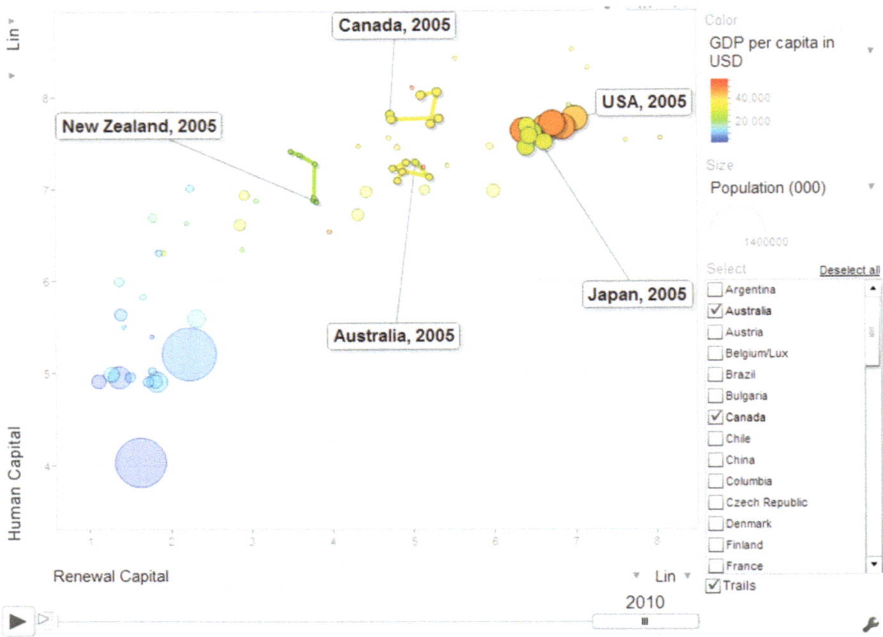


**Fig. 3.14** Human capital versus renewal capital for Australia, Canada, Japan, New Zealand, and the USA

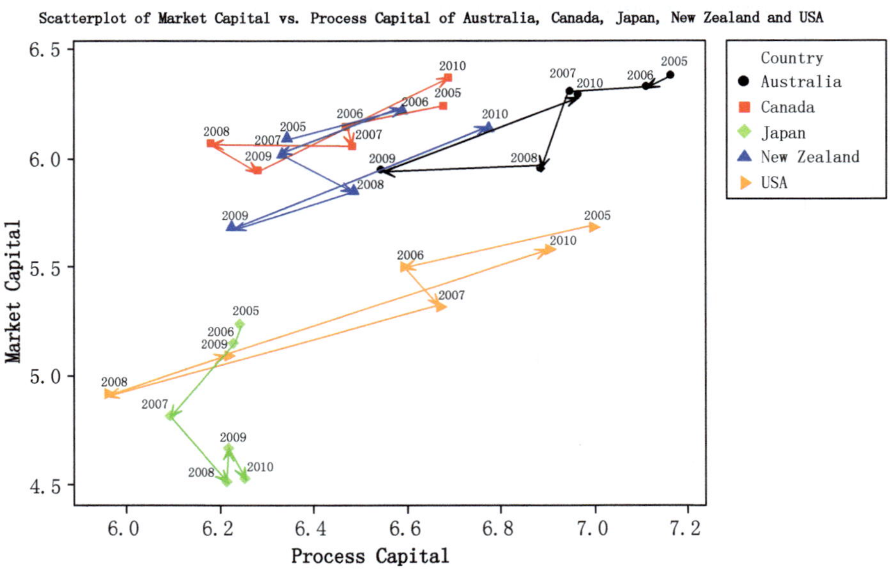


**Fig. 3.15** A scatterplot of market capital versus process capital for Australia, Canada, Japan, New Zealand, and the USA

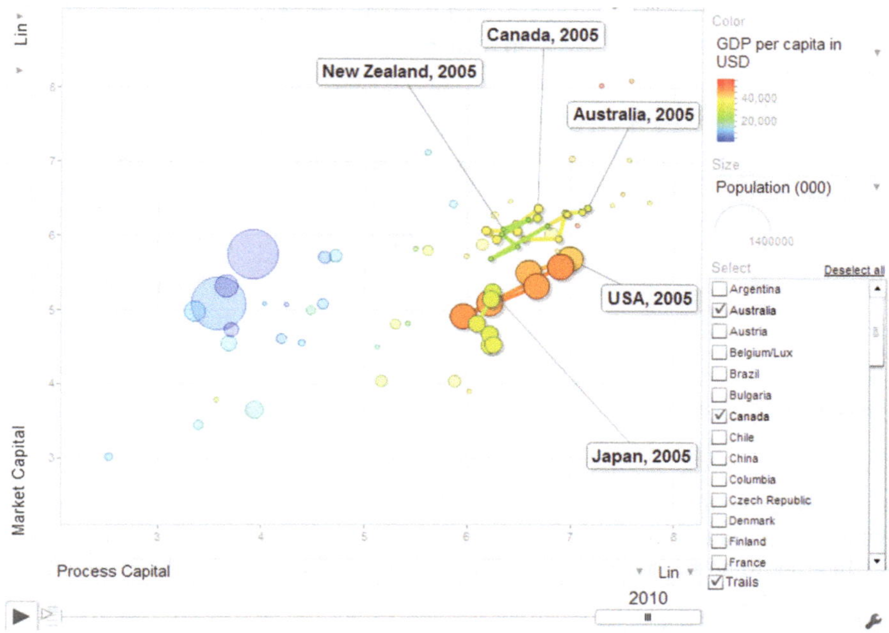


**Fig. 3.16** Market capital versus process capital for Australia, Canada, Japan, New Zealand, and the USA

capitals that can be expected to produce faster results if a nation is willing to engage in more extensive investments.

Figure 3.15 particularly shows the relatively large fluctuation of the short-term NIC before and after the financial crisis. Australia clearly leads the short-term NIC, although it started to decline from 2006 and rebounded in 2009. New Zealand has good progress in its short-term NIC over the years. In 2010, Canada and the USA were largely returning to their 2005 strength, with Canada having a little improvement and the USA a little decline. Japan is the lowest in the short-term NIC, with continuous market capital decreases. In general, Fig. 3.16 shows that these five countries have better process capital than market capital on the 48-country world map.

## Dynamics of National Intellectual Capital in Three Time Periods

The illustrations and graphs in the previous section describe the internal progression of NIC in each country (Figs. 3.1–3.6) and the path of development of various capitals (Figs. 3.8–3.12). The ranking changes that will be introduced in this section

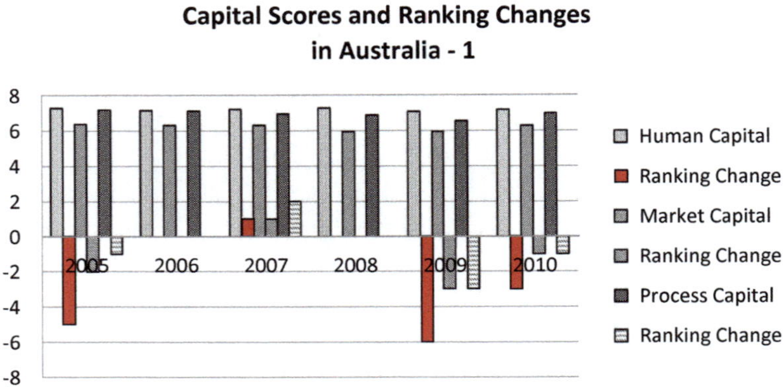


**Fig. 3.17** Human capital, market capital, process capital, and ranking changes in Australia

represent external competitiveness. Rankings, by and large, is a zero-sum game in which the advance of one country simultaneously marks the decline of another.

In order to probe the dynamics of NIC change before and after the financial crisis, we plotted Figs. 3.17, 3.18, 3.19, 3.20, 3.21, 3.22, 3.23, 3.24, 3.25, and 3.26 and Table 3.2 in three time periods: 2005–2006, 2007–2008, and 2009–2010. To have a clearer presentation, we separate the data into two sets. The first set contains capital scores and ranking changes of human capital, market capital, and process capital in Figs. 3.17, 3.19, 3.21, 3.23, and 3.25. The second set exhibits capital scores and ranking changes of renewal capital, financial capital, and average NIC in Figs. 3.18, 3.20, 3.22, 3.24, and 3.26.

The figures are mapped based on the mean capital scores and ranking changes of each period. Ranking changes in Figs. 3.17–3.26 are next to each capital score and copied from the bold-faced ranking difference of columns 2, 5, 7, and 9 of Table 3.2. Taking the human capital ranking difference for Australia (−5, 1, −6, −3), for example, the ranking change of "−5," representing the difference between the third period (2009–2010) and first period (2005–2006), is plotted at 2005; the ranking change of "1," representing the difference between the second period (2007–2008) and first period (2005–2006), is plotted at 2007; the ranking change of "−6," representing the difference between the third period (2009–2010) and second period (2007–2008), is plotted at 2009; and the ranking change of "−3," representing the difference between the third period (2009–2010) and 6-year average ranking (exhibited in Table 3.1), is plotted at 2010. Special attention can be paid to the negative numbers, which indicate that the level of a particular capital was higher before than after the financial crisis. As it is easier to read figures than tables, we will describe the findings of each figure separately.

As shown in Fig. 3.17 and Table 3.2, Australia's human capital (−5, 1, −6, −3) showed relatively large ranking declines. Negative five (−5) and negative six (−6) ranks in human capital mean Australia was losing its human capital international competitiveness after the financial crisis. When comparing its ranking in 2009–

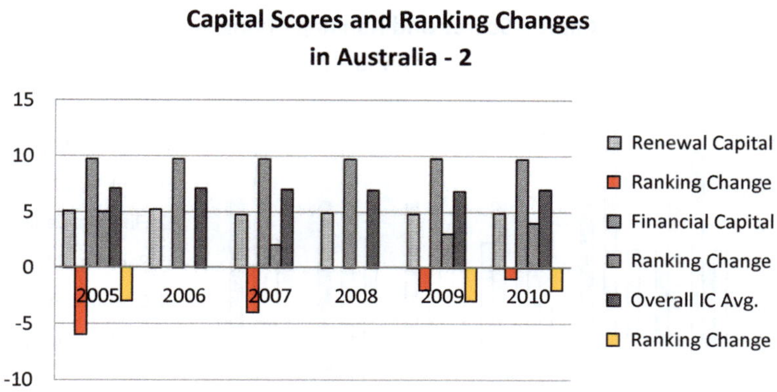


**Fig. 3.18** Renewal capital, financial capital, average NIC, and ranking changes in Australia

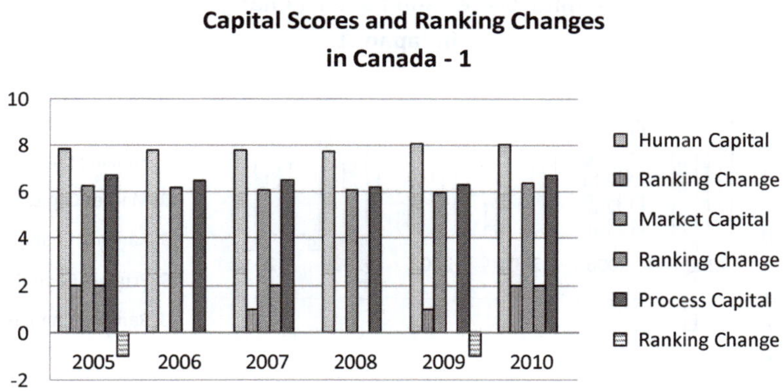


**Fig. 3.19** Human capital, market capital, process capital, and ranking changes in Canada

2010 with that of the 6-year average (plotted at 2010), it dropped by three ranks (−3). The negative numbers of its ranking changes in market capital (−2, 1, −3, −1) and process capital (−1, 2, −3, −1) also show that Australia has been competed down internationally in these two areas after the financial crisis. Even though Fig. 3.17 shows that its market capital score did not have much difference between the years 2007–2008 (6.31 and 5.95) and 2009–2010 (5.95 and 6.29), its ranking still dropped (−3). This means that maintaining internal stability does not guarantee external competitiveness. Therefore, attending to both NIC internal score and external competitiveness, pertinent changes are suggested.

Figure 3.18 shows that Australia's renewal capital (−6, −4, −2, −1) and NIC (−3, 0, −3, −2) were losing international competitiveness during and after the

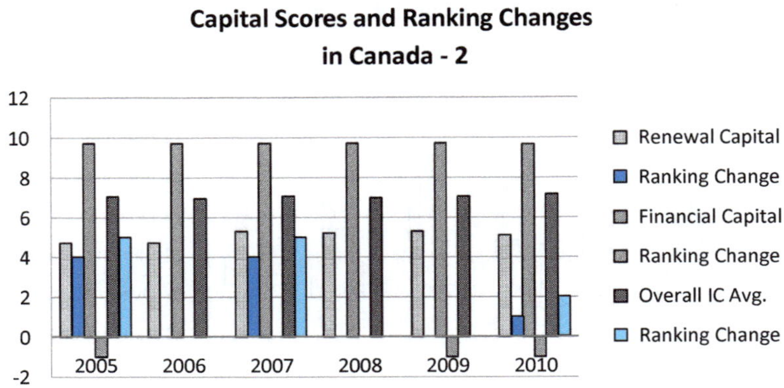


**Fig. 3.20** Renewal capital, financial capital, average NIC, and ranking changes in Canada

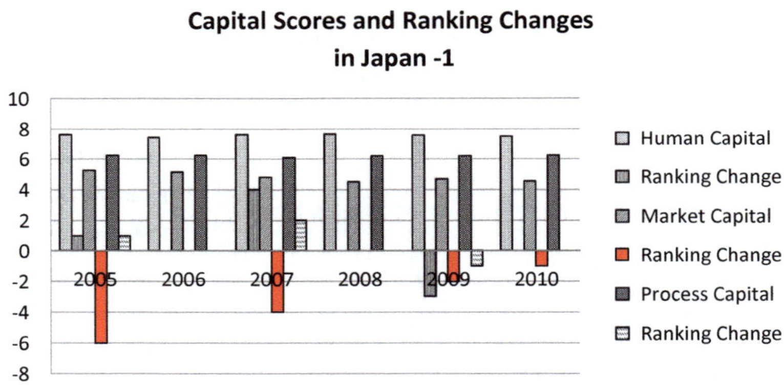


**Fig. 3.21** Human capital, market capital, process capital, and ranking changes in Japan

financial crisis; however, its financial capital ranking (5, 2, 3, 4) improved over the three time periods.

Figure 3.19 shows that all four types of human capital (2, 1, 1, 2) and market capital (2, 2, 0, 2) ranking comparisons in Canada are positive, indicating that Canada was gaining international competitiveness in these two areas after the financial crisis. Although its process capital (−1, 0, −1, 0) ranking changes have two negative numbers, the change is relatively small. Figure 3.20 shows that Canada had relatively large-scale ranking gains in renewal capital (4, 4, 0, 1) and average NIC (5, 5, 0, 2), indicating its increasing international competitiveness in these two areas after the financial crisis. Its financial capital (−1, 0, −1, −1) had a minor decrease.

Figure 3.21 shows that Japan experienced a relatively large-scale and all negative ranking change in market capital (−6, −4, −2, −1), with only one negative num-

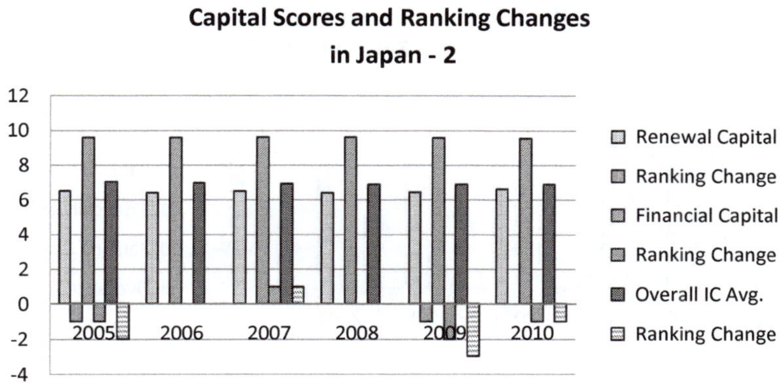


**Fig. 3.22** Renewal capital, financial capital, average NIC, and ranking changes in Japan

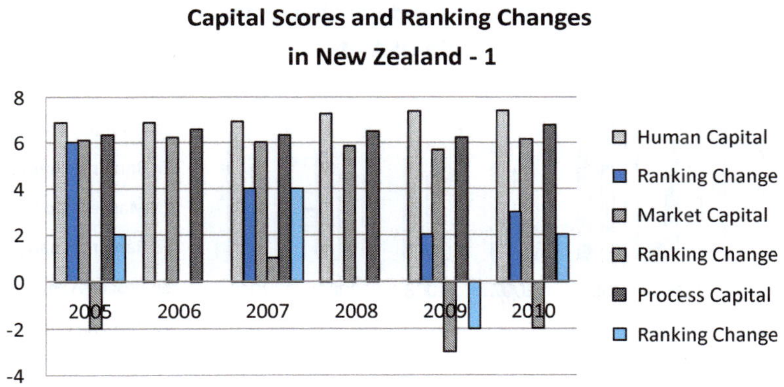


**Fig. 3.23** Human capital, market capital, process capital, and ranking changes in New Zealand

ber in human capital (1, 4, −3, 0) and process capital (1, 2, −1, 0). That is, Japan was losing its market capital international competitiveness after the financial crisis. Figure 3.22 indicates that Japan had more negative than positive ranking changes in renewal capital (−1, 0, −1, 0), financial capital (−1, 1, −2, −1), and average NIC (−2, 1, −3, −1), although their scale of change is relatively small. Overall, Japan lost intangible NIC international competitiveness after the financial crisis.

Figure 3.23 shows that New Zealand exhibited relatively large-scale ranking gains in human capital (6, 4, 2, 3) and process capital (2, 4, −2, 2), even though its process capital regressed two ranks in the third comparison. However, New Zealand largely experienced ranking declines in market capital (−2, 1, −3, −2), indicating that it lost international competitiveness after the financial crisis. Figure 3.24 indicates that New Zealand had a minor ranking loss in renewal capital (0, 1, −1, 0),

**Fig. 3.24** Renewal capital, financial capital, average NIC, and ranking changes in New Zealand

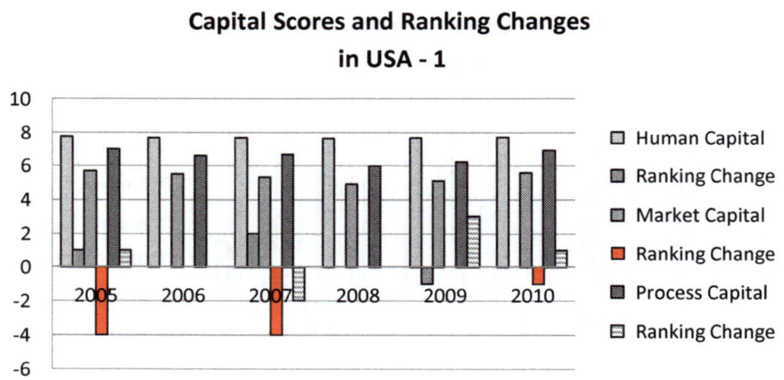


**Fig. 3.25** Human capital, market capital, process capital, and ranking changes in the USA

financial capital (−2, −1, −1, 0), and average NIC (0, 1, −1, 0) after the financial crisis.

Figure 3.25 shows that the USA had more ranking gains than loss in human capital (1, 2, −1, 0) and process capital (1, −2, 3, 1). However, it experienced relatively large-scale ranking declines in market capital (−4, −4, 0, −1), indicating that it lost market capital international competitiveness after the financial crisis. Figure 3.26 shows that the USA had very minor ranking changes in renewal capital (−1, 0, −1, −1) and average NIC (1, 0, 1, 0). There was no ranking change at all for its financial capital.

In summary, for human capital, Australia showed a downward trend, New Zealand a large-scale upward trend, and Canada a small-scale upward trend. For market

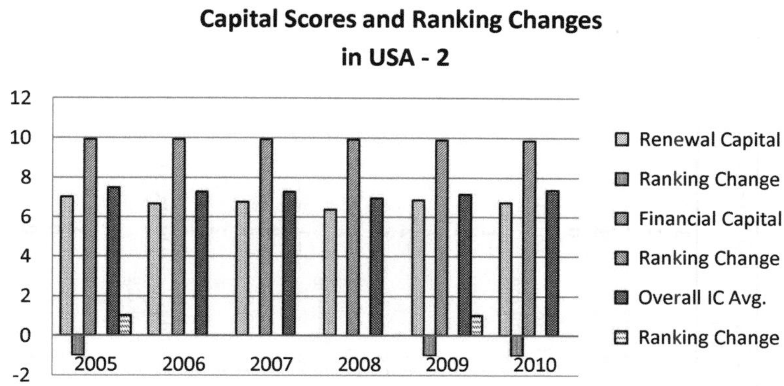


**Fig. 3.26** Renewal capital, financial capital, average NIC, and ranking changes in the USA

capital, Japan had the largest-scale ranking decline, followed by the USA, New Zealand, and Australia. Canada is the only country that had market capital ranking gains for all four comparisons. For process capital, all five countries had ranking gains and losses, although on a small scale. Overall, New Zealand had relatively large-scale ranking gains.

For renewal capital, Australia had a relatively large-scale ranking decline, whereas Canada had relatively large-scale ranking gains. The ranking changes of the other three countries are relatively small. For financial capital, Australia had the largest ranking gains and the USA did not have any ranking change over the three time periods. Ranking changes of the other three countries were relatively small. For NIC, Australia had relatively large-scale ranking declines, followed by Japan. On the contrary, Canada had relatively large-scale ranking gains.

Taking a cursory look at Figs. 3.17–3.26, Australia had the largest number of rank declines and Canada had the largest number of rank gains. That is, Australia lost its NIC international competitiveness, whereas Canada increased its NIC international competitiveness post financial crisis.

## 3D NIC Trajectory

Up until this section, Figs. 3.1–3.26 plotted different combinations of various types of capital, capital–GDP codevelopment, and ranking changes on a 2D plane. Even though Figs. 3.7–3.12 displayed four dimensions with color and bubble size as the third and fourth dimensions in addition to the *X*- and *Y*-axis, graphically they are still on one plane. This section presents 3D graphs showing each country's NIC development trajectory on a 48-country 3D landscape of various types. As NIC

**Table 3.2** Ranking changes in three time periods for Australia, Canada, Japan, New Zealand, and the USA

| | (First period–third period) | First period 2005–2006 | Second period 2007–2008 | | Third period 2009–2010 | | Third period ranking vs. overall NIC ranking | |
|---|---|---|---|---|---|---|---|---|
| Human capital | Difference#1 | Ranking | Ranking | Difference | Ranking | Difference | NIC 48 ranking | Difference |
| Australia | **−5** | 13 | 12 | **1** | 18 | **−6** | 15 | **−3** |
| Canada | **2** | 6 | 5 | **1** | 4 | **1** | 6 | **2** |
| Japan | **1** | 11 | 7 | **4** | 10 | **−3** | 10 | **0** |
| New Zealand | **6** | 21 | 17 | **4** | 15 | **2** | 18 | **3** |
| USA | **1** | 8 | 6 | **2** | 7 | **−1** | 7 | **0** |
| Market capital | Difference | Ranking | Ranking | Difference | Ranking | Difference | NIC 48 ranking | Difference |
| Australia | **−2** | 11 | 10 | **1** | 13 | **−3** | 12 | **−1** |
| Canada | **2** | 13 | 11 | **2** | 11 | **0** | 13 | **2** |
| Japan | **−6** | 29 | 33 | **−4** | 35 | **−2** | 34 | **−1** |
| New Zealand | **−2** | 15 | 14 | **1** | 17 | **−3** | 15 | **−2** |
| USA | **−4** | 22 | 26 | **−4** | 26 | **0** | 25 | **−1** |
| Process capital | Difference | Ranking | Ranking | Difference | Ranking | Difference | NIC 48 ranking | Difference |
| Australia | **−1** | 9 | 7 | **2** | 10 | **−3** | 9 | **−1** |
| Canada | **−1** | 14 | 14 | **0** | 15 | **−1** | 15 | **0** |
| Japan | **1** | 19 | 17 | **2** | 18 | **−1** | 18 | **0** |
| New Zealand | **2** | 16 | 12 | **4** | 14 | **−2** | 16 | **2** |
| USA | **1** | 13 | 15 | **−2** | 12 | **3** | 13 | **1** |
| Renewal capital | Difference | Ranking | Ranking | Difference | Ranking | Difference | NIC 48 ranking | Difference |
| Australia | **−6** | 11 | 15 | **−4** | 17 | **−2** | 16 | **−1** |
| Canada | **4** | 17 | 13 | **4** | 13 | **0** | 14 | **1** |
| Japan | **−1** | 6 | 6 | **0** | 7 | **−1** | 7 | **0** |
| New Zealand | **0** | 22 | 21 | **1** | 22 | **−1** | 22 | **0** |
| USA | **−1** | 5 | 5 | **0** | 6 | **−1** | 5 | **−1** |

**Table 3.2** (continued)

| | (First period–third period) | First period 2005–2006 | Second period 2007–2008 | | Third period 2009–2010 | | Third period ranking vs. overall NIC ranking | |
|---|---|---|---|---|---|---|---|---|
| Human capital | Difference#1 | Ranking | Ranking | Difference | Ranking | Difference | NIC 48 ranking | Difference |
| Financial capital | Difference | Ranking | Ranking | Difference | Ranking | Difference | NIC 48 ranking | Difference |
| Australia | **5** | 12 | 10 | **2** | 7 | **3** | 11 | **4** |
| Canada | **−1** | 9 | 9 | **0** | 10 | **−1** | 9 | **−1** |
| Japan | **−1** | 19 | 18 | **1** | 20 | **−2** | 19 | **−1** |
| New Zealand | **−2** | 24 | 25 | **−1** | 26 | **−1** | 26 | **0** |
| USA | **0** | 3 | 3 | **0** | 3 | **0** | 3 | **0** |
| NIC | Difference | Ranking | Ranking | Difference | Ranking | Difference | NIC 48 ranking | Difference |
| Australia | **−3** | 12 | 12 | **0** | 15 | **−3** | 13 | **−2** |
| Canada | **5** | 15 | 10 | **5** | 10 | **0** | 12 | **2** |
| Japan | **−2** | 14 | 13 | **1** | 16 | **−3** | 15 | **−1** |
| New Zealand | **0** | 21 | 20 | **1** | 21 | **−1** | 21 | **0** |
| USA | **1** | 8 | 8 | **0** | 7 | **1** | 7 | **0** |

The second column compares the third period (2009–2010) ranking with the first period (2005–2006)
The fifth column compares the second period (2007–2008) ranking with the first period (2005–2006)
The seventh column compares the third period (2009–2010) ranking with the second period (2007–2008)
The last column compares the most current third period (2009–2010) ranking with the original 6-year average NIC48 ranking summarized in Table 3.1

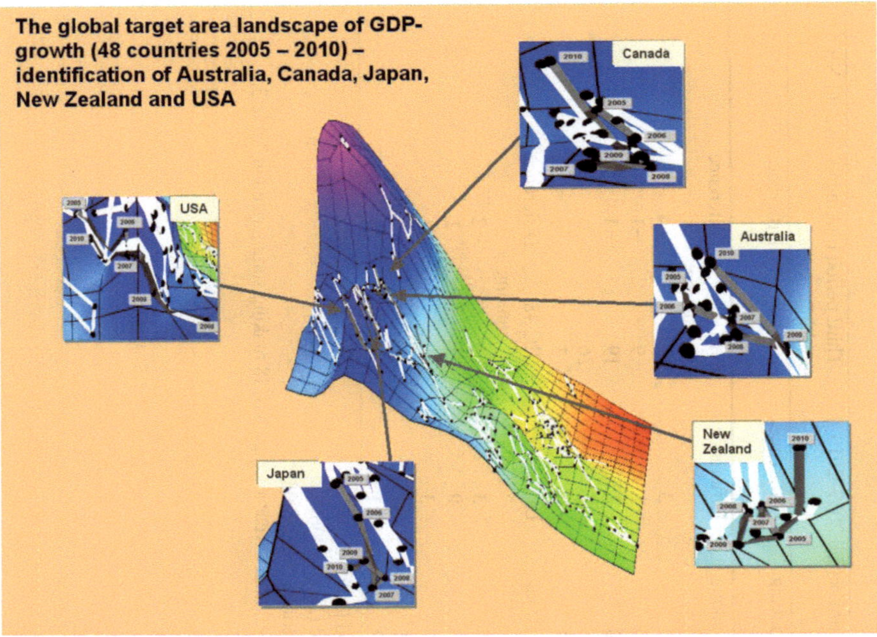


**Fig. 3.27** The NIC trail of Australia, Canada, Japan, New Zealand, and the USA on a 3D 48-country landscape

evolution over time is always complex, combining different views from different angles may provide more comprehensive perspectives for analysis.

In what follows, we first explore the value-driving context by uncovering the path of GDP growth for Australia, Canada, Japan, New Zealand, and the USA from 2005 to 2010. Second, in explaining the GDP growth, we present the high, middle, and low capabilities which human capital, market capital, process capital, and renewal capital, respectively, have. Third, we examine the efficiency (GDP growth)-enhancing and -impeding factors of each economy, taking each economy's turning point into consideration. Last, we identify the efficiency drivers of each economy in reaching a targeted GDP.

Figure 3.27 shows a rectangular 3D landscape, with a longer north–south side. The formation of the landscape is based on the data of 29 NIC indicators (presented in Appendix 3) for 48 countries covering 6 years (2005–2010), with a total of 8,352 ($29 \times 48 \times 6$) data points. In other words, Fig. 3.27 is the aggregated NIC landscape of the 48 countries. The enlarged trails in Fig. 3.27 indicate NIC progression (upward), regression (downward), or configuration change (sideward) of each economy over the 6-year period. Each white trail on the landscape represents a country. The altitude coloring from purple, dark blue, blue, green, yellow, to red is computer generated, according to GDP values, with purple representing high GDP

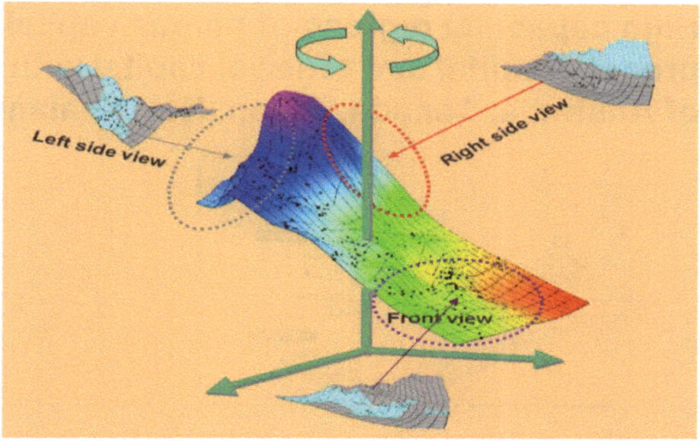


**Fig. 3.28** The potential rotation and partial presentation of the 3D formation

and red low GDP. Figure 3.28 presents the potential rotation or partial presentation of the 3D formation in order to provide readers a better view of the focal area of discussion.

The relative NIC positions of Australia, Canada, Japan, New Zealand, and the USA (pointed out with arrows) are located at the upper left-hand side of the overall 3D landscape.

Figures 3.29, 3.30, and 3.31 form a set. The areas of focus are shaded in light blue. Automated by the computer program to have a better view, the three figures are taken from a frontal-left view as Fig. 3.28 indicates. Figure 3.29 presents four graphs indicating the high-capability region of human capital, market capital, process capital, and renewal capital in explaining the GDP growth. High capability means the data points are 20 % above the mean value of each capital. The figure shows that most of the four capitals in these five countries are in the high-capability region, except the market capital of Japan.

Figure 3.30 displays another four graphs indicating the middle-capability region of each human capital, market capital, process capital, and renewal capital in explaining the GDP growth. Middle capability means the data points are within the top 50 % value of each capital. The figure shows that Japan's market capital is in the middle-capability region.

Figure 3.31 presents the last four graphs in this set and indicates the low-capability region of each human capital, market capital, process capital, and renewal capital in explaining the GDP growth. Low capability means the data points are 20 % below the mean value of each capital. The figure shows that none of the capital in these five countries is in the low-capability region.

In general, Figs. 3.29–3.31 as a set explain that 95 % of the capitals (19 out of $4 \times 5 = 20$) of these five countries are in the high-capability region in explaining GDP growth. These three figures demonstrate that these five advanced countries are relatively competitive in national intangible assets among the 48 countries. In an era when intangible assets play an increasingly important role in the national

**Fig. 3.29** The high-capability region of human capital, market capital, process capital, and renewal capital

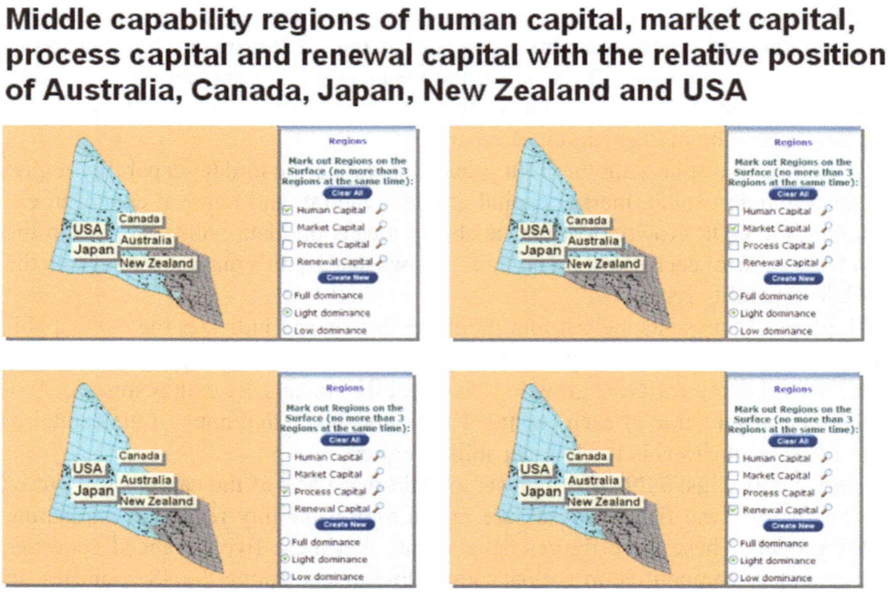


**Fig. 3.30** The middle-capability region of human capital, market capital, process capital, and renewal capital

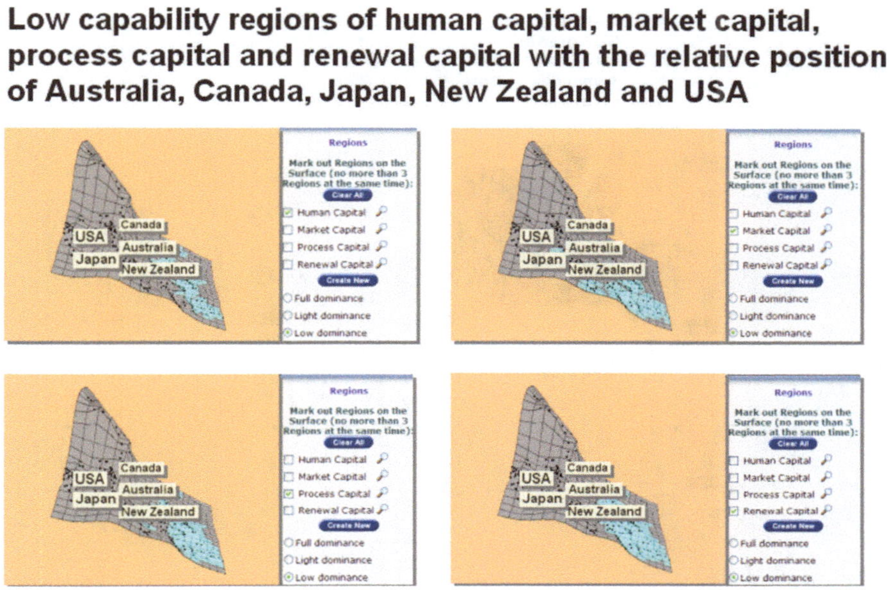


**Fig. 3.31** The low-capability region of human capital, market capital, process capital, and renewal capital

development, the messages revealed in these graphs deserve special attention for interested parties.

Another set of figures, Figures 3.32, 3.33, 3.34, 3.35, and 3.36 display efficiency-enhancing or -impeding factors that affect GDP growth before and after the NIC turning point for Australia, Canada, Japan, New Zealand, and the USA, respectively. The white indicator boxes at the upper right display the results of the enhancing or impeding factors. All the five countries had one NIC turning point; therefore, we employed three rounds of data analysis. For instance, Australia's turning point is 2009; therefore, we traced the explaining factors of 2005 against 2009 (starting point → the turning point), 2008 against 2009 (1 year before the turning point → the turning point), and 2009 against 2010 (the turning point → the ending point).

For an easy reference, we summarize in Table 3.3 two sets of results, each with the five key factors. If there is a clear percentage difference cutting point (such as less than 1 % in the white indicator boxes), the reported factors may be less than five. The results for the first set show the efficiency-enhancing and -impeding factors before the turning point. The results for the second set show the efficiency-enhancing and -impeding indicators after the turning point in italic letters. As the factor strength (percentage) varies with different explaining power, we also calculated the average weight of the five enhancing and impeding factors and display each respective percentage in the rows for "Factor #5." We then count the frequency of four more frequently displayed categories, namely government-related issues (G), human capital-related issues (H), market capital-related issues (M), and R&D issu-

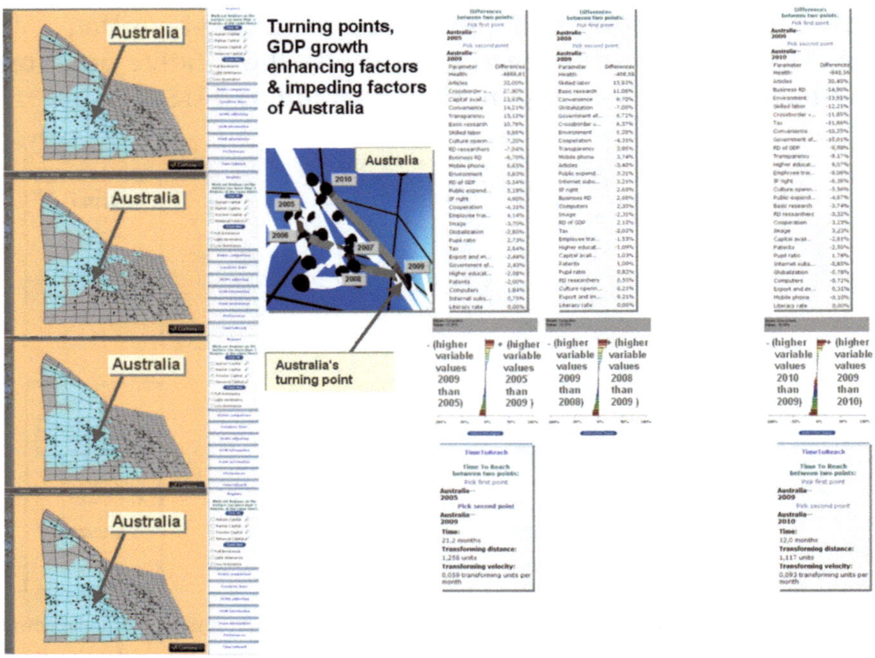


**Fig. 3.32** Turning point and GDP growth-enhancing and -impeding factors of Australia

es. Because capital availability was a concern during the financial crisis, we particularly highlighted this factor as "G-C."

Figure 3.32 shows the 2009 turning point and the enhancing and impeding factors of Australia. The four 3D graphs on the left-hand side of the figure indicate that all Australia's human capital, market capital, process capital, and renewal capital fall into the high-capability region (20 % above average).

Table 3.3 shows that in Australia, R&D-related issues consist of the main enhancing factors. However, 4 of the 5 counts were before the turning point, with a relatively light explaining weight of 5.46 %. Nevertheless, business R&D investment was an enhancing factor before and after the turning point. On the contrary, scientific article was an impeding factor before and after the turning point. Government-related issues had more counts as an impeding factor than other categories. Capital availability was the third impeding factor before the turning point, reflecting Australia's financial stress before 2009 even though the country weathered the crisis pretty well. Two other government issues—convenience of establishing new firms and transparency of government policy—were impeding factors before the turning point with a relatively large explaining weight of 22.23 %. A good sign in Australia is that cross-border ventures changed from an impeding factor before the turning point to an enhancing factor after the turning point. On the contrary, the factor "image of country" developed in the opposite direction. After the 2009 turning

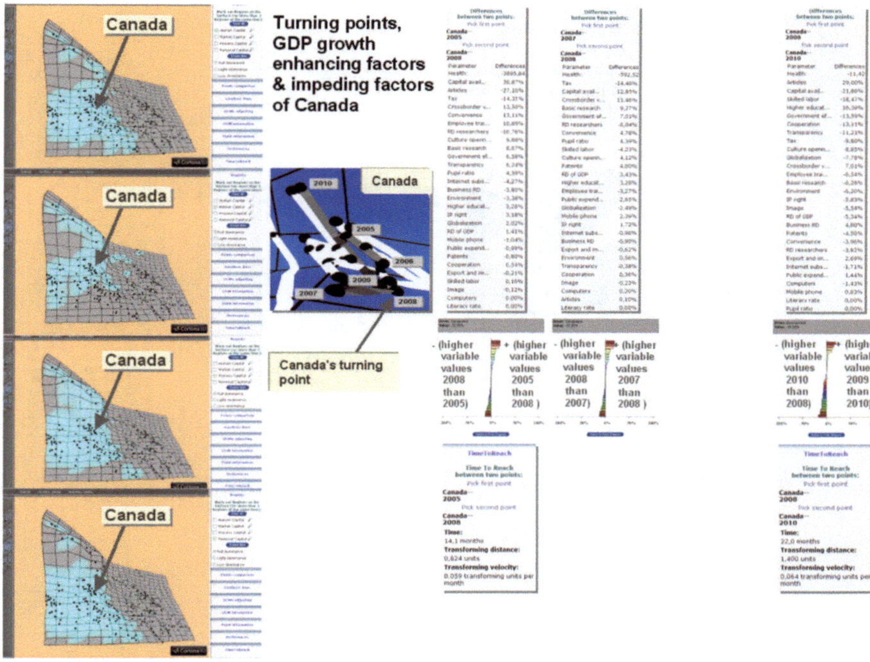


**Fig. 3.33** Turning point and GDP growth-enhancing and -impeding factors of Canada

point, the explaining weights of enhancing and impeding factors are relatively even with 12.91 and 11.12%, respectively. Special attention may be paid to the first two impeding factors after the 2009 turning point—scientific articles and higher education enrollment, which may help improve Australia's declining ranking in human capital and renewal capital as exhibited in Table 3.2.

In Fig. 3.33, Canada's turning point is the year 2008. The four 3D graphs on the left-hand side indicate that its human capital, market capital, process capital, and renewal capital are in the high-capability region (20% above average). Table 3.3 shows that government-related issues and R&D issues constitute the major counts of enhancing factors, with 4 counts each. Market capital-related issues have the largest counts as impeding factors, including cross-border ventures, openness of culture, and export of goods. Specifically, its capital availability improved from an impeding factor before the turning point to an enhancing factor after the turning point, reflecting its stabilized financial situation after 2008. For Canada, "cross-border ventures" remained an impeding factor before and after the turning point. In addition, its scientific articles and business R&D investment changed from enhancing factors before the turning point to impeding factors after the turning point. For Canada, the explaining weight of enhancing and impeding factors before and after its turning point is relatively even, ranging from 11.94 to 15.65%.

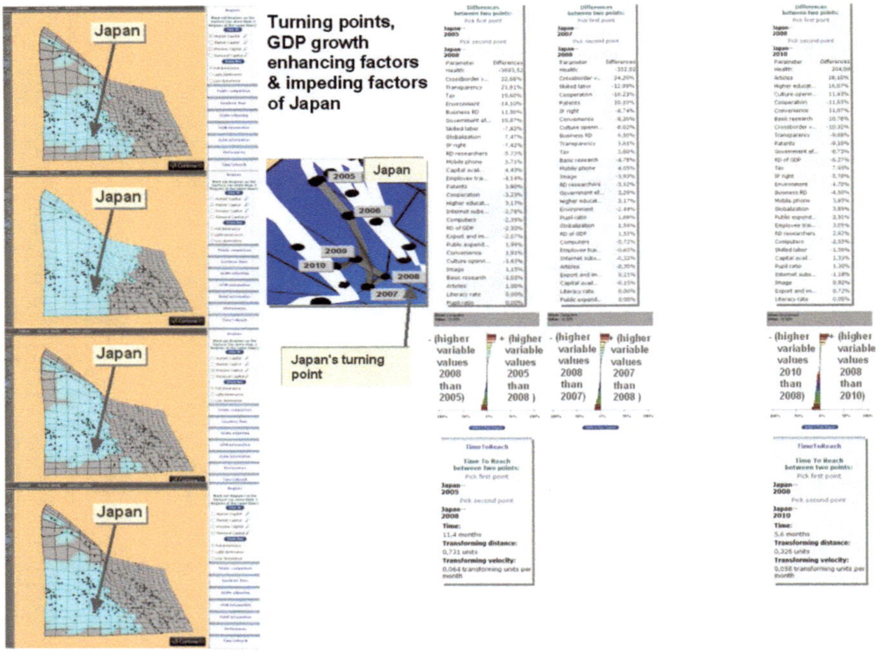


**Fig. 3.34** Turning point and GDP growth-enhancing and -impeding factors of Japan

Figure 3.34 shows 2008 as Japan's NIC turning point. The four 3D graphs on the left-hand side of the figure indicate that human capital, process capital, and renewal capital for Japan are in the high-capability region (20 % above average), yet its market capital is in the middle-capability region (top 50 %). Table 3.3 shows that R&D-related issues have the largest count (5 counts) of enhancing factors, whereas government-related issues (also 5 counts) explain a major part of impeding factors. There are two good signs: cross-border ventures and transparency of government policy improved from impeding factors before the turning points to enhancing factors after the turning point. However, corporate tax encouragement remained an impeding factor before and after the turning point. As the explaining weight of impeding factors before the turning point is relatively high (17.31 %), the impeding factors of corporate tax encouragement, business R&D investment, and government efficiency deserve some attention. The other two impeding factors before the turning point have been improved to enhancing factors after the turning point, mentioned above. Special attention may be paid to the two market capital-related impeding factors—cross-border ventures and openness of culture. The finding agrees with Japan being criticized as less open to foreign-directed investment and foreign culture.

Figure 3.35 shows 2009 as New Zealand's turning point. The four 3D graphs on the left-hand side of the figure indicate that all four capitals for New Zealand are in

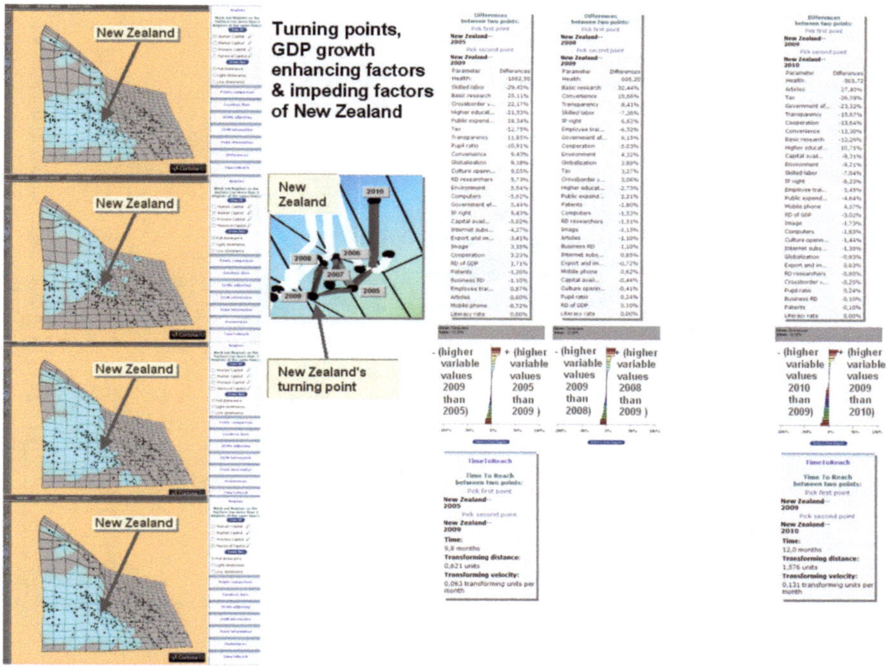


Fig. 3.35 Turning point and GDP growth-enhancing and -impeding factors of New Zealand

the high-capability region (20 % above average). Table 3.3 shows that government-related issues (4 counts) and human capital-related issues (3 counts) constitute the major enhancing factors. There is no distinctive category that explains a major part of its impeding factors. In New Zealand, corporate tax encouragement remains an enhancing factor before and after the turning point. There are two good signs: transparency of government policy and convenience of establishing new firms improved from impeding factors before the turning point to enhancing factors after the turning point. After the turning point, only three impeding factors are over 1 % explaining weight, indicating New Zealand's relatively stable NIC status after 2009. Yet, some attention may be paid to the first two impeding factors after the turning point—scientific articles and higher education enrollment, which may help improve its long-term NIC as exhibited in Fig. 3.13. For New Zealand, the explaining weight of enhancing and impeding factors before and after its turning point is relatively even, ranging from 14.23 to 18.30 %.

Figure 3.36 shows 2008 as the USA's turning point. The four 3D graphs on the left-hand side of the figure indicate that all four capitals for the USA are in the high-capability region (20 % above average). Table 3.3 shows that government-related issues constitute the major part of the enhancing factors as well as impeding factors, both 4 counts. Before the turning point, the explaining weight of enhancing factors

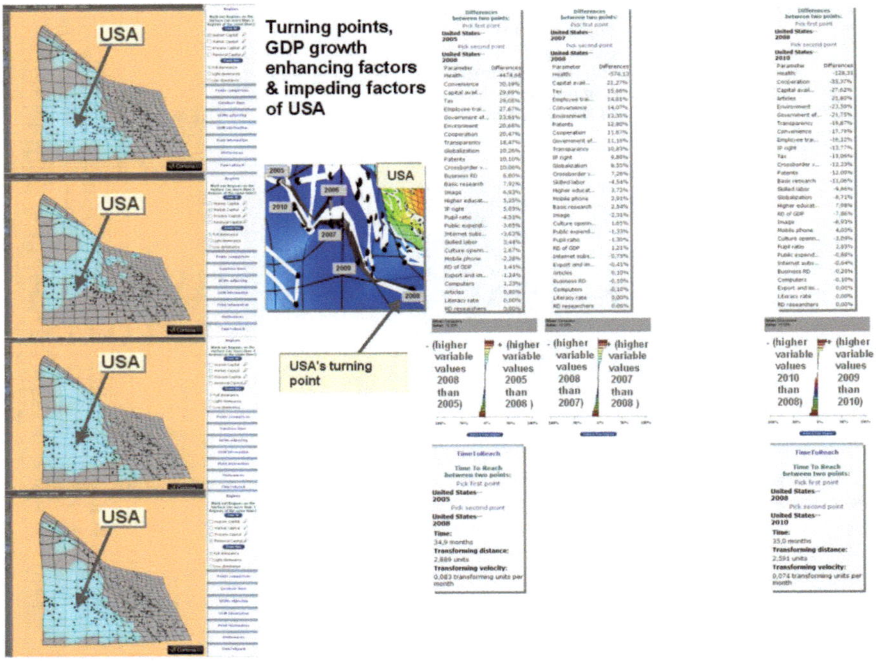


**Fig. 3.36** Turning point and GDP growth-enhancing and -impeding factors of the USA

(3.06 %) is much less than that of impeding factors (28.05 %). There are two good signs. Capital availability and government efficiency improved from impeding factors before the turning point to enhancing factors after the turning point, explaining the likely effect of the government stimulus packages and disbursement. However, both mobile phone subscribers and pupil–teacher ratio turned from enhancing factors before the turning point to impeding factors after the turning point. As the explaining weight of enhancing factors after the turning point is quite high (25.62 %), the following five enhancing factors deserve some recognition: university–enterprise cooperation, capital availability, fair business competition environment, government efficiency, and transparency of government policies. For the USA, the gaps of explaining weight of enhancing and impeding factors before and after its turning point are relatively large, ranging from 3.06 to 28.05 %.

To summarize Table 3.3 into an overall suggestion, we count the frequency of both enhancing and impeding factors by categories for all five countries, shown in the last row of the table. There are a total of 32 counts of government-related issues (G), including 4 counts of capital availability, among which there are 16 counts each of enhancing and impeding factors. For the 16 counts of government-related enhancing factors, Canada, New Zealand, and the USA have 4 counts each, indicating that their public policies are relatively good. For the 16 counts of government-related

**Table 3.3** Enhancing factors and impeding factors of GDP per capita (ppp) growth for the five advanced countries

| Influencing factor | Australia | | Canada | | Japan | | New Zealand | | USA | |
|---|---|---|---|---|---|---|---|---|---|---|
| | Enhancing factors | Impeding factors | Enhancing factors | Impeding factors | Enhancing factors | Impeding factors | Enhancing factors | Impeding factors | Enhancing factors | Impeding factors |
| Factor #1 before the turning point | R&D researchers (R&D) | Scientific articles (R&D) | Scientific articles (R&D) | Capital availability (G-C) | Fair business competition environment (G) | Cross-border ventures (M) | Skilled labor (H) | Basic research (R&D) | Pupil–teacher ratio (H) | Convenience of establishing new firms (G) |
| *Factor#1 after the turning point* | *Business R&D* (R&D) | *Scientific articles* (R&D) | *Capital availability* (G-C) | *Scientific articles* (R&D) | *University–enterprise cooperation* (R&D) | *Scientific articles* (R&D) | *Corporate tax encouragement* (G) | *Scientific articles* (R&D) | *University–enterprise cooperation* (R&D) | *Scientific articles* (R&D) |
| Factor #2 before the turning point | Business R&D (R&D) | Cross-border ventures (M) | Corporate tax encouragement (G) | Cross-border ventures (M) | Skilled labor (H) | Transparency of government policy (G) | Higher education enrollment (H) | Cross-border ventures (M) | Public expenditure on education (H) | Capital availability (G-C) |
| *Factor #2 after the turning point* | *Fair business competition environment* (G) | *Higher education enrollment* (H) | *Skilled labor* (H) | *Higher education enrollment* (H) | *Basic research* (R&D) | *Higher education enrolment* (H) | *Government efficiency* (G) | *Higher education enrollment* (H) | *Capital availability* (G-C) | *Higher education enrollment* (H) |

**Table 3.3** (continued)

| Influencing factor | Australia | | Canada | | Japan | | New Zealand | | USA | |
|---|---|---|---|---|---|---|---|---|---|---|
| | Enhancing factors | Impeding factors | Enhancing factors | Impeding factors | Enhancing factors | Impeding factors | Enhancing factors | Impeding factors | Enhancing factors | Impeding factors |
| Factor #3 before the turning point | R&D % GDP (R&D) | Capital availability (G-C) | R&D researchers (R&D) | Convenience of establishing new firms (G) | IP rights protection (R&D) | Corporate tax encouragement (G) | Corporate tax encouragement (M) | Public expenditure on education (H) | Internet subscribers | Corporate tax encouragement (G) |
| *Factor #3 after the turning point* | *Skilled labor* (H) | *Image of country* (M) | *Government efficiency* (G) | *Cross-border ventures* (M) | *Cross-border ventures* (M) | *Openness of culture* (M) | *Transparency of government policy* (G) | *Mobile phone subscribers* | *Fair business competition environment* (G) | *Mobile phone subscribers* |
| Factor #4 before the turning point | University–enterprise cooperation (R&D) | Convenience of establishing new firms (G) | Internet subscribers | Employee training (H) | R&D researchers (R&D) | Business R&D (R&D) | Pupil–teacher ratio (H) | Transparency of government policy (G) | Mobile phone subscribers | Employee training (H) |
| *Factor #4 after the turning point* | *Cross-border ventures* (M) | *Pupil–teacher ratio* (H) | *University–enterprise cooperation* (R&D) | *Business R&D* (R&D) | *Transparency of government policy* (G) | *Convenience of establishing new firms* (G) | *University–enterprise cooperation* (R&D) | – | *Government efficiency* (G) | *Pupil–teacher ratio* (H) |

**Table 3.3** (continued)

| Influencing factor | Australia | | Canada | | Japan | | New Zealand | | USA | |
|---|---|---|---|---|---|---|---|---|---|---|
| | Enhancing factors | Impeding factors | Enhancing factors | Impeding factors | Enhancing factors | Impeding factors | Enhancing factors | Impeding factors | Enhancing factors | Impeding factors |
| Factor #5 before the turning point | Image of country (M) | Transparency of government policy (G) | Business R&D (R&D) | Openness of culture (M) | Employee training (H) | Government efficiency (G) | R&D researchers (R&D) | Convenience of establishing new firms (G) | Export of goods (M) | Government efficiency (G) |
| | **(Average explaining power—5.46 %)#** | **(Average explaining power—22.23 %)** | **(Average explaining power—12.04 %)** | **(Average explaining power—15.65 %)** | **(Average explaining power—7.84 %)** | **(Average explaining power—17.31 %)** | **(Average explaining power—16.07 %)#** | **(Average explaining power—17.38 %)** | **(Average explaining power—3.06 %)** | **(Average explaining power—28.05 %)** |
| *Factor #5 after the turning point* | *Corporate tax encouragement* (G) | – | *Transparency of government policy* (G) | *Export of goods* (M) | *Patents* (R&D) | *Corporate tax encouragement* (G) | *Convenience of establishing new firms* (G) | – | *Transparency of government policy* (G) | – |
| | **(Average explaining power—12.91 %)** | **(Average explaining power—11.12 %)** | **(Average explaining power—15.65 %)** | **(Average explaining power—11.94 %)** | **(Average explaining power—10.34 %)** | **(Average explaining power—13.02 %)** | **(Average explaining power—18.30 %)** | **(Average explaining power—14.23 %)** | **(Average explaining power—25.62 %)** | **(Average explaining power—10.17 %)** |

**Table 3.3** (continued)

| Influencing factor | Australia | | Canada | | Japan | | New Zealand | | USA | |
|---|---|---|---|---|---|---|---|---|---|---|
| | Enhancing factors | Impeding factors | Enhancing factors | Impeding factors | Enhancing factors | Impeding factors | Enhancing factors | Impeding factors | Enhancing factors | Impeding factors |
| Category frequency count | G—2<br>H—1<br>M—2<br>R&D—5 | G—3<br>H—2<br>M—2<br>R&D—2 | G—4<br>H—1<br>M—0<br>R&D—4 | G—2<br>H—2<br>M—4<br>R&D—2 | G—2<br>H—2<br>M—1<br>R&D—5 | G—5<br>H—1<br>M—2<br>R&D—2 | G—4<br>H—3<br>M—1<br>R&D—2 | G—2<br>H—2<br>M—1<br>R&D—2 | G—4<br>H—2<br>M—1<br>R&D—1 | G—4<br>H—3<br>M—0<br>R&D—1 |
| Category frequency count—**grand total** | G—16<br>H—9<br>M—5<br>R&D—17 | G—16<br>H—10<br>M—9<br>R&D—9 | | | | | | | | |

(*G*) and (*G-C*) government-related issues including capital availability represented by G-C (total 32 counts including 4 counts of capital availability)
(*H*) human capital issues (19 counts)
(*M*) market capital issues (14 counts)
(*R&D*) research and development (26 counts)

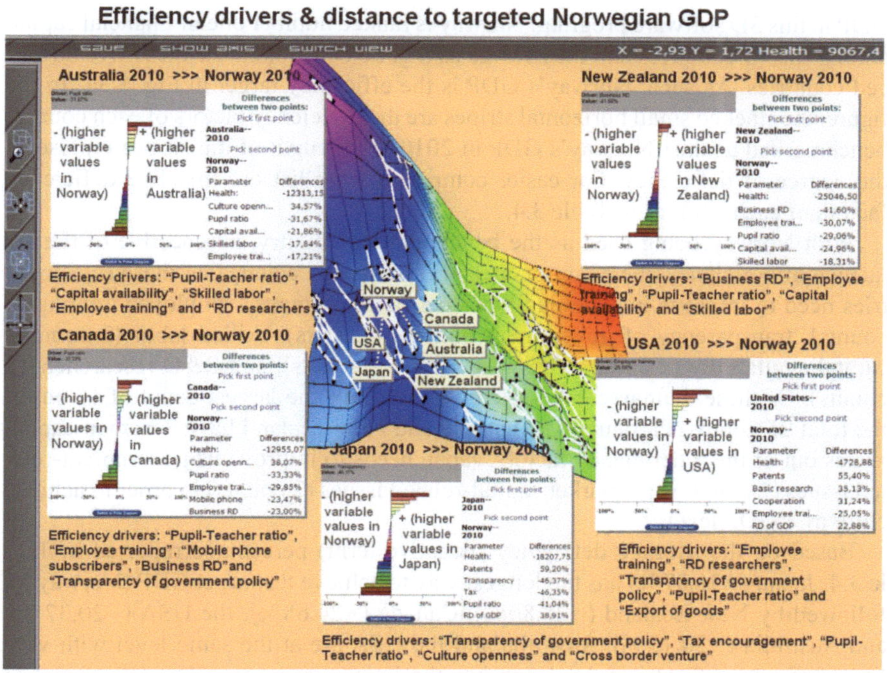


**Fig. 3.37** Efficiency drivers and distance to targeted GDP of Norway

impeding factors, Japan has 5 counts, followed by the USA with 4 counts and Australia with 3 counts.

There are 19 counts of human capital issues (H), among which 10 counts are impeding factors, with the USA having the largest count of three, including higher education enrollment, employee training, and pupil–teacher ratio. There are 14 counts of market capital issues (M), among which 9 counts are impeding factors, with Canada having the largest count of 5, including 2 counts of cross-border ventures, openness of culture, and export of goods. For R&D issues, there are 26 counts, among which impeding factors make up only total 9 counts. That is, 17 counts of R&D issues are enhancing factors, with Australia and Japan having 5 counts each, followed by Canada with 4 counts. Seemingly, these five advanced countries have utilized their R&D relatively well as enhancing factors.

For enhancing factors, the average explaining weights before the turning point were smaller than those after the turning point for all five countries, indicating a more positive effect of these enhancing factors after either 2008 or 2009. On the contrary, for impeding factors, the average explaining weights before the turning point were higher than those after the turning point for all five countries, representing more stress brought about by these impeding factors before the turning point.

Figure 3.37 identifies the efficiency drivers (positive term) for each individual country. Efficiency targeting is similar to benchmarking. Efficiency represents the

GDP in this 3D software program. Norway is ranked number one in financial capital among the 48 countries and thus serves as a good benchmark for these five advanced countries. As such, Norway's GDP is the efficiency target in Fig. 3.37. In the figure, the stacked small horizontal stripes are the deficiency factors of each country benchmarked against Norway's GDP in 2010. The length of the stripes represents the degree of deficiency. For easier comparison, we list the first five deficiency factors of each country in Table 3.4.

With Norway being used as the benchmarking country, irrespective of the sequence of deficiency, the common areas (in frequency count) that these five countries need to improve include pupil–teacher ratio (5 counts), employee training (4 counts), transparency of government policy (3 counts), skilled labor (2 counts), capital availability (2 counts), business R&D (2 counts), and R&D researchers (2 counts). Of these, human capital-related issues have the largest count of 11 out of the total 25 counts. Particularly, Australia and New Zealand have 3 human capital issues out of the 5 deficiency factors. Japan needs to improve its government-related issues (2 counts) and market capital-related issues (2 counts) in order to achieve Norway's GDP level.

Based on the average deficiency (negative term) percentage reported in Table 3.4, Japan (−36.07 %) has the longest way to achieve the target GDP (Norway's), followed by New Zealand (−28.80 %), Canada (−24.68 %), the USA (−20.37 %), and Australia (−20.15 %). Australia and the USA are at the same level with very little difference. Surprisingly, Japan has the longest route to achieve the level of Norway's GDP, even though its NIC is better than New Zealand.

The added value of the above 3D trajectory analysis is to: 1) display the NIC trails of the discussed countries on a 48-country landscape; 2) locate the capability region of the four individual capitals for each country; 3) highlight the NIC turning point, the details of the enhancing or impeding factors, and the dynamics of factor changes for each country; and 4) calculate the distance that each country has to progress in order to achieve the benchmark GDP and identify the first five key factors to reach this goal. This section supplements the previous sections by looking into the contribution of each individual indicator in each year, rather than from the perspective of average scores and average rankings.

In this chapter, we have reported our research findings in layman's terms with graphs and tables of various types for easier reading. This study on national intangible assets has uncovered some important findings that are not apparent in other GDP-related studies. For instance, Japan has the longest way to achieve the level of Norway's GDP, even though it outperforms New Zealand in most of the indicators. In addition, its global competitiveness ranked by the World Economic Forum was much higher than that of New Zealand (9 vs. 25) in 2011–2012. Such findings pose an interesting point for further exploration concerning Japan's future national well-being.

**Table 3.4** The first five efficiency drivers targeting GDP of Norway

| Efficiency driver | Australia | Canada | Japan | New Zealand | USA |
|---|---|---|---|---|---|
| Factor #1 | Pupil–teacher ratio | Pupil–teacher ratio | Transparency of government policy | Business R&D | Employee training |
| Factor #2 | Capital availability | Employee training | Corporate tax encouragement | Employee training | R&D researchers |
| Factor #3 | Skilled labor | Mobile phone subscribers | Pupil–teacher ratio | Pupil–teacher ratio | Transparency of government policy |
| Factor #4 | Employee training | Business R&D | Openness of culture | Capital availability | Pupil–teacher ratio |
| Factor #5 | R&D researchers | Transparency of government policy | Cross-border ventures | Skilled labor | Export of goods |
| Average deficiency percentage of the above five drivers | −20.15 % | −24.68 % | −36.07 % | −28.80 % | −20.37 % |

# Chapter 4
# Beyond the 2008 Global Financial Crisis

## Australia

Australia came through the recession relatively unscathed, maintaining good levels of business investment and employment (Heritage 2012). It was one of the first advanced economies to recover from the financial crisis and to raise interest rates, with seven rate hikes between October 2009 and November 2010 (CIA 2012). The following three main reasons explain why the Australian economy did better than almost all other advanced economies. First, the Australian government and Reserve Bank of Australia had timely policy responses to this global financial crisis; second, the Australian economy trades substantially with Asia and, in particular, China, thus benefiting from Chinese growth in the midst of this highly synchronized global slowdown; and third, the Australian banking system has sound regulations and remained in good shape throughout the crisis (Kennedy 2009).

According to the Organisation for Economic Co-operation and Development (OECD), Australia's timely stimulus measures, with a strong focus on direct government investment, are among the most effective of all OECD fiscal packages in stimulating activity and supporting employment (Treasurer 2009). Australia learned important lessons from its past two recessions in the early 1980s and 1990s, especially regarding how stimulus packages should be planned and the design of policies to support the unemployed. Statistics show that with the stimulus, about 210,000 more people had jobs and around 60% of these new jobs were full time (Kennedy 2009; ILO 2010a).

Overall, Australia's economic performance since the onset of this global financial crisis has been stronger than anticipated. Much of the contraction in labor demand in 2008–2009 took the form of declines in average working hours rather than increases in unemployment (ILO 2010a). Furthermore, its strong prudential and

C. Y.-Y. Lin et al., *National Intellectual Capital and the Financial Crisis in Australia, Canada, Japan, New Zealand, and the United States,* SpringerBriefs in Economics,
DOI 10.1007/978-1-4614-9308-2_4, 

corporate reporting framework was a key reason why the country did not see the collapse of any major financial institution (Treasurer 2009). With robust supervision and sound regulations, the Australian banking system coped well with the financial turmoil, and the government's budget deficit was much lower than those of other major economies (Heritage 2012). Its government debt of 22.31 % of its GDP in 2010 (Fig. 2.2) was the lowest among the five countries reported in this volume.

Up to 2010, much of the impetus for Australia's growth came from fiscal and monetary stimulus. However a private sector recovery also took hold, with the export volumes increasing by 1.7 % in the fourth quarter of 2009 and the terms of trade rose by 2.9 %. The outlook for private business investment improved, as business confidence rebounded and profitability recovered in 2010 (ILO 2010a).

As of 2012, temporary stimulus measures have largely been phased out (Heritage 2012). Australia's GDP grew by 3.3 % in 2010. Unemployment, originally expected to reach 8–10 %, peaked at 5.7 % in late 2009 and fell to around 5 % in 2010 (Fig. 2.3). As a result of an improved economy, the budget deficit is expected to be below 4.2 % of the GDP and the government is expected to return to budget surpluses as early as 2015 (CIA 2012).

## Canada

In Canada, major banks, among the strongest in the world, emerged from the 2008 global financial crisis, owing to the financial sector's tradition of conservative lending practices and strong capitalization (CIA 2012). Job gains returned in January 2010 with an additional 43,000 jobs added to the economy, however, mostly in part-time work. In the same month, the unemployment rate stood at 8.3 %, down 0.2 percentage points from December 2009 and slightly below its peak of 8.6 % in October 2009. Nonetheless, youth unemployment in January 2010 stood at 15.1 %, up by 2 percentage points from a year before (ILO 2010b). General government debt as a percentage of GDP increased from around 71 % in 2008 to 84.05 % in 2010 (Fig. 2.2). During 2010, Canada's economy grew only 3 %, due to decreased global demand and a highly valued Canadian dollar (CIA 2012). The OECD (2012a) predicted that the main drivers of growth in Canada would be private consumption and investment and projected its growth to be around 2.25 % in 2012 and 2.5 % in 2013.

Many reasons contributed to Canada's weathering the crisis well, including lessons learned from its painful reforms in the 1980s and early 1990s, a relatively fiscally conservative government, and the prudent nature of Canadians. Therefore, while other nations borrowed, Canada had a budget surplus for over a decade (Hepker 2010). Canada's "Economic Action Plan" was put forth during the financial crisis, targeting a short-term stimulus as well as long-term national growth. Specifically, Canadian stimulus measures consist of reducing taxes permanently, enhancing employment insurance and training programs for the unemployed, strengthening the work-sharing program to avoid layoffs, creating jobs through a massive injection of infrastructure spending, improving infrastructure at colleges and universities with special supports for research and technology, supporting industries and communities most affected by the global downturn, and improving access to and the affordability of financing for Canadian households and businesses (Government of Canada 2012). As a result, the confidence of Canadians was restored after its government invested in the Economic Action Plan without incurring a permanent deficit. Canada's relatively low debt burden has allowed the government to make permanent tax reductions in support of its long-term economic growth, while other countries have provided only temporary relief (Government of Canada 2012).

According to the Department of Finance Canada (2011), the introduction of Canada's Economic Action Plan was timely and its implementation on track. With a US$ 48.8 billion (C$ 60 billion) fiscal stimulus package to steer an effective recovery, close to US$ 26 billion (C$ 32 billion) support was provided to individuals and businesses most affected by the economic downturn in 2009–2010. An additional US$ 22.8 billion (C$ 28 billion) was to be delivered in 2010–2011. Through the Plan, more than 26,000 projects have been completed or are underway. These projects continuously put Canadians to work across the country and have contributed to a strong labor market recovery since July 2009.

Up to fiscal year 2010–2011, the following projects and stimulus values were spent and allocated (Dept. of Finance Canada 2011). It is to be noted that the stimulus values are from the Canadian government's official website and should be in Canadian dollars, which have been converted to US dollars for the consistency of our report. The major plans and values by 2010–2011 include: reducing the tax burden for Canadians US$ 5.8 billion (C$ 6.2 billion), helping the unemployed US$ 7.8 billion (C$ 8.3 billion), building infrastructure to create jobs US$ 13.9 billion (C$ 14.8 billion), advancing Canada's knowledge economy and creating better jobs US$ 3.6 billion (C$ 3.8 billion), supporting industries and communities US$ 12.4 billion (C$ 13.2 billion), and taking provincial and territorial actions US$ 13.2 billion (C$ 14 billion).

The following reasons may explain why Canadian banks did well during the crisis (Porter 2010). Canada has a strong prudential bank regulator—the Office of the Superintendent of Financial Institutions Canada (OSFI). OSFI requires Canadian banks to hold 7 % of Tier 1 capital and 10 % total capital, above the Basel II requirements of 4 % and 8 %—the highest among the G7 countries. Moreover, OSFI insists on high-quality Tier 1 capital, that is, 75 % or more must be common equity. During the crisis, the Canadian government introduced an Insured Mortgage Purchase Program (IMPP) in October 2008, which allocated US$ 105.9 billion (C$ 125 billion) of its 2009 budget to purchase securitized mortgages from banks (Nadeau 2009). With stricter regulations and government support, Canadian banks have avoided more of the excessively aggressive market practices than were rampant in the USA and other jurisdictions that were harder hit by the crisis.

As of 2011, Canada has more than fully recouped all its loss in output experienced during the recession and its economy has posted the strongest employment growth among the G7 countries since June 2009 (Dept. of Finance Canada 2011).

## Japan

Japan started off with relative insulation from the US sub-prime crisis and the early stages of the global financial crisis (Wei 2009). The prudent lending behavior of Japanese banks has helped Japan avoid a debt-driven housing price bubble (Jones and Tsutsumi 2009). The implementation of Basel II, announced in 2004, reduced banks' appetite for risk; as a result, the capital weight of mortgages fell from 35–50% to as low as 15–20% for banks (Jones and Tsutsumi 2009). In addition, the remuneration system and corporate governance in Japan do not promote a risk-taking behavior as they do in many countries. In contrast to the 1990s' crisis, this time the response of the Japanese government was prompt and forceful (Jones and Tsutsumi 2009), which helped the economy withstand the external financial shock relatively well.

In fiscal year 2009–2010, Japan posted its first trade surplus of US$ 54.2 billion (¥ 5.23 trillion) after the financial crisis. However, it continued to be troubled by deflation, high public debts, weak domestic demand, softening exports, and a strong yen (Japanese currency). In 2010, growth for the first quarter and the second quarter was 1.2% and 0.1% respectively, due to cooling exports and flat domestic growth (Hays 2011). In March 2010, the Japanese government pushed a record US$ 1 trillion (¥ 92.3 trillion) budget through the Parliament aimed at stimulating growth in the long-stagnant economy (Hays 2011). Anticipating the global economic slowdown, in May 2010 (the month Greece had its first bailout) the Bank of Japan injected US$ 21.6 billion (¥ 2 trillion) to stabilize markets. In August 2010, Japanese stock index, the Nikkei, sunk to a 9-month low and 10-year Japanese government bonds yields fell below 1%.

To further revive the economy, in September 2010 the Japanese government approved a US$ 1.1 billion stimulus package for buying energy-efficient appliances, subsiding environmentally friendly and energy-saving sectors, providing funds for building overseas factories to ease the impact of the yen's rise, and supporting employment for new college graduates and the jobless (Hays 2011). At the same time, the government also proposed a stimulus package of US$ 6 billion that focused on job creation, economic growth, social welfare, revitalizing regional economies, and deregulation, of which US$ 1.3 billion was for child care support and other social welfare programs and US$ 350 million for job creation (Hays 2011). In addition, the government also proposed that child allowances be raised to US$ 233 (¥ 20,000) per month from US$ 152 (¥ 13,000) for children under 3 years and the regional government be given more discretion on how they use state funds (Hays 2011).

In the third quarter of 2010, the Japanese economy expanded by 4.5% due mainly to the pump-priming measures, with consumer spending. In November 2010, the Nikkei closed above 10,000 for the first time in 5 months, mainly powered by the strong performance of Japanese banks, a slight weakening of the yen, and strong exports. In December 2010, the Japanese government proposed major tax reforms for fiscal 2011 that covered cutting corporate income tax from 40 to 35%, introducing an environmental tax in October 2011, lowering the corporate tax rate for small businesses from 18 to 15%, and limiting deductions from taxable incomes of high-income workers and corporate executives (Hays 2011). Although Japan's economy contracted 1.3% in the fourth quarter of 2010, it expanded 3.9% over the year compared with the previous year, signaling a recovery from the recession that came in the wake of the global economic crisis (Hays 2011).

Growth in fiscal 2010–2011 (from April 2010 to April 2011) was 3.1%. Unemployment was around 5%. Exports were up by 24%, the first rise in 3 years, mainly supported by strong demand from China and other emerging economies in Asia. By early 2011, Japan's exports were accelerating, the unemployment rate was falling, and confidence was rising (Gurria 2011). However, Japan's net exports and export competitiveness were hurt by a surge in the yen and growth in fiscal 2011–2012 was predicted to be 1.5% (Hays 2011).

Unfortunately, the great east Japan earthquake struck just when Japan's economy was getting back on track and gaining momentum after a slowdown in the later part of 2010. A 9.0-magnitude earthquake and an ensuing tsunami devastated the northeast coast of Honshu Island on March 11, 2011, killing thousands, severely damaging several nuclear power plants, and displacing and leaving homeless more than 320,000 people with a million households without running water (CIA 2012). Estimated direct costs of the damage range from US$ 235 billion to US$ 310 billion. With the disaster, Japan's GDP for 2011 was predicted to decline by as much as 1% for the year (CIA 2012). In fact, the aftereffect was much worse than expected. Its GDP growth in 2011 was −0.7%, down from over 4% in 2010; however, it bounced to 2% in 2012 (Global Finance 2013a).

Overall, Japan was dragged into an economic slowdown in 2010 until the third quarter, but then the earthquake of March 2011 further delayed its return to financial stability and growth.

## New Zealand

New Zealand's economic recovery began promisingly in mid-2009 and benefited from growing trade linkages to China and other emerging markets in Asia. Dairy and other food prices surged as rising living standards in such populous markets have boosted demands from New Zealand. The country also benefited from its high degree of economic integration with robust Australia (OECD 2011d). As a result, New Zealand emerged from the global economic turmoil relatively unscathed with modest growth resuming from the second quarter of 2009 and a pull out of recession in late 2009 (Treasury 2010; CIA 2012). Household saving became positive (0.2% of household disposable income) in March 2011 for the first time since 2000, mainly due to uncertainty about global developments and their impact on New Zealand. Firms were also more cautious about growth prospects and delayed some employment and investment plans (Treasury 2012). Public debt, increased by crisis for which above 20% of its GDP had to be spent, was still moderate compared to other advanced countries (Heritage 2012).

However, growth lost momentum by the second half of 2010 as the global economy slowed and households and firms remained cautious with their spending, despite record terms of trade and support from policy stimulus. New Zealand's recovery has been weaker than previously thought. Therefore, its annual growth rate in March 2011/2012 was adjusted to 1.9 % (down from 2.3 %) and real GDP growth in March 2012/2013 was projected to be 2.8 % (down from 3.4 %) (Treasury 2012). In addition, a strong earthquake that struck the Canterbury region in September 2010 also contributed to stagnation in activities in the second half of the year. A second and more damaging earthquake in late February 2011 (centered on Christchurch) further retarded the recovery in 2011 and made the outlook highly uncertain (OECD 2011d).

However in the first half of 2012, positive impact from the World Cup in late 2011 and the assumed ramp-up of rebuilding in Canterbury from late 2012 proved helpful. The earthquake-related rebuilding was expected to provide substantial impetus to economic activity in coming years, even though the aftershocks were likely to delay some rebuilding by one to two quarters (Treasury 2012).

In 2012, continuing sovereign debt concerns in the Euro zone increased global risk aversion. There were also signs of slower growth and lower forecasts elsewhere, including China and other parts of Asia (Treasury 2012). The likely price fall for New Zealand's commodity exports, reduced manufacturing and tourism from weaker global demand, a relatively high exchange rate, and funds from overseas becoming more expensive and difficult to obtain all impede its recovery.

The main supports to New Zealand's future growth would be low interest rates, comparatively strong growth of its two main trading partners—Australia and China—and the rebuilding of the Canterbury region (OECD 2012b). Reconstruction (officially estimated at 8 % of its GDP) is projected to get fully underway in 2012 and provide a substantial boost to demand over a number of years (OECD 2011d). Therefore, growth is expected to be higher in 2013/2014 than previously expected.

Although its unemployment rate was 6.6 % in the September 2011/2012 quarter, wages and hours worked were stronger. In the medium term, the deficit will rise above 6 % of its GDP, owing partly to the increase in investment and the rebuilding in Canterbury. In 2012, risks to the economic outlook remained skewed to the downside as there was a possibility of much worse outcomes for the Euro area (Treasury 2012).

The Treasury of New Zealand has predicted economic growth to rise to 1.6 % in March 2012, 2.6 % in 2013, and 3.4 % in 2014. However, New Zealand's household consumption is expected to slow down to 2.2 % in 2013 from 2.7 %, as the Rugby World Cup effect fades (McBeth 2012). The Treasury's forecasts assume New Zealand's net migration will turn positive in 2014 as the country's economy outperforms Australia and the Christchurch rebuild attracts workers from overseas.

## The United States

After the global financial crisis, the US economy continues to recover. Nevertheless, the adverse effects of the crisis are still being felt, particularly in the form of lasting high unemployment. Although year-over-year GDP growth forecast in the fourth quarter of 2010 was between 2.5% and 3.3%, the economy continued to shed jobs and the labor market remained weak (ILO 2010d). In January 2010, the number of long-term unemployed (those jobless for 27 weeks or more) continued to rise, reaching 6.3 million, or 40% of total unemployment, and the number of discouraged workers grew to over 1 million (ILO 2010d). In the same month, the US government proposed new measures to assist small businesses access more credit and receive tax help to create private sector jobs. In addition, public investments were increased in infrastructure, science, technology, and research (ILO 2010d).

In March 2010, a health insurance reform bill was passed, which will extend coverage to an additional 32 million American citizens by 2016, through private health insurance for the general population and Medicaid for the impoverished. In July 2010, the White House signed the DODD-FRANK Wall Street Reform and Consumer Protection Act to promote financial stability by protecting consumers from financial abuses, ending taxpayer bailouts of financial firms, dealing with troubled banks that are "too big to fail," and improving accountability and transparency in the financial system (CIA 2012). The bill, in particular, requires certain financial derivatives to be traded in markets that are subject to government regulation and oversight (CIA 2012).

In 2010, households as well as companies in the USA rebuilt their balance sheets with the household savings rate increasing (Falke 2010). Regarding the US$ 787 billion fiscal stimulus, approximately two-thirds of these funds were injected into the economy by the end of 2010. The same year, the US budget deficit shot up to 10% of the GDP (Falke 2010). Total government revenues from taxes and other sources remained lower, as a percentage of GDP, than that of any other developed country. Nevertheless, the economic recovery has gained momentum since the first half of 2011, with moderate employment gains and a pick-up in the pace of consumer spending (OECD 2012d). Housing demand has increased noticeably, but the overhang of unsold homes and the tide of foreclosures still strain the revival in residential investment (OECD 2012d).

By early 2011, much of the funds supported by the Troubled Asset Relief Program (TARP) in late 2008 had been returned to the US government from banks and other industrial corporations (CIA 2012). As the economy is still overcoming important hurdles, real GDP growth is projected to increase only gradually in 2012 and 2013 (OECD 2012d). With very large budget deficits and fast-rising federal debt, an agreement on a credible medium-term fiscal consolidation program becomes increasingly urgent as the economy continues to recover (OECD 2011e). Measures such as restricting tax expenditures would lower the deficit while reducing market distortions and narrowing income inequality (OECD 2012d).

The OECD (2012c) suggested that legislative decisions and a gradual pace should be considered to avoid the fiscal "cliff" in 2013 due to the scheduled expiration of tax cuts and automatic spending cuts. The IMF estimated that the fiscal costs of the US sub-prime crisis may tally about US$ 1.4 trillion, or around 11 % of its GDP (Reinhart and Rogoff 2008). To build a more resilient economy, banking institutions should be encouraged to maintain high levels of equity capital. Furthermore, efforts to develop improved analytical tools and information systems to monitor risks to the financial system should be enhanced.

For the effect of the stimulus package, the US$ 787 billion package has created or secured 3.6 million jobs, according to the White House (Falke 2010).

# Chapter 5
# Future Perspectives and Policy Implications

By the middle of 2013, more than 4 years have passed since the outbreak of the 2008 global financial crisis. Although some countries in the European Union (EU) are still in financial trouble, it is time to reflect upon what happened during the past few years and what can be learned from this crisis for future prevention.

After the financial crisis, global recovery started from 2010. However, it stagnated in the second half of 2011, mainly due to sovereign debt problems in Europe and a modest recovery in the USA. In January 2012, the International Monetary Fund (IMF) announced that the global recovery was threatened by intensifying strains in the Euro area; thus, financial conditions have deteriorated, growth prospects have dimmed, and downside risks have escalated (IMF 2012). The Euro area economy went into a mild recession in 2012. The effects of bank deleveraging on the real economy may surface again and the impact of additional fiscal consolidation may heighten. Even growth in developing economies that had traditionally remained resilient was expected to slow down because of the worsening external environment and a weakening of internal demand (IMF 2012).

However, as of mid-2013, signs of stronger recovery have surfaced in the USA and the economic prospect in Japan also became promising with Minister Abe's financial relaxing policy, although in January 2012, the World Bank (2012) projected only 2.5 % growth for 2012. In fact, the statistics of January 2013 showed that the world economy in 2012 grew by 3.7 %, with the Euro area at 0.7 %, advanced countries 2 %, and developing Asia 8.1 % (Global Finance 2013b). However, affected by the European market slowdown, China grew by 9.2 % in 2011 and 8.2 % in 2012 (Global Finance 2013a). These numbers reveal that, in the years to come, there are promising prospects as well as challenges to which world leaders need to pay close attention.

In this chapter, we first present the prospects of these five advanced countries (Australia, Canada, Japan, New Zealand, and the USA) and then describe their potential challenges in the future. The prospects and challenges are meant to provide

C. Y.-Y. Lin et al., *National Intellectual Capital and the Financial Crisis in Australia, Canada, Japan, New Zealand, and the United States,* SpringerBriefs in Economics,
DOI 10.1007/978-1-4614-9308-2_5, © The Author(s) 2014

points of thought for discussion and they do not represent an exhaustive list. This chapter concludes with some policy implications.

## Prospects

During this global financial crisis, the contraction, rise in unemployment, and regulatory reforms can be viewed as the necessary restructuring costs for transitioning from the existing economy to an even more robust one (Lo 2009). Countries weathered this crisis well, such as Australia and Canada, reported that they learned valuable lessons from previous crises. Therefore, the next several years will be extremely challenging and important for future implications. In the wake of the crisis, closer supervision, adaptive and functional regulatory changes, and structural reforms will be implemented in most countries. Such actions will support and create new infrastructures for future growth and prosperity in a better way. As each individual country has its own systems and resources, we briefly describe the prospects of each country as follows.

### *Australia*

In addition to Australia's proven resilience during this financial crisis, the following prospects may help the country build an even more robust economy.

1. Australia is aggressively engaged in the Trans-Pacific Partnership talks and ongoing free trade agreement negotiations with China, Japan, and Korea (CIA 2012).
2. Australia's abundant and diverse natural resources including coal, iron ore, copper, and gold continue to attract high levels of foreign investment.
3. Australia was ranked the third freest economy in the world in 2011. The country has a strong tradition of openness to global trade and investment with transparent and efficient regulations. Its independent judiciary helps protect property rights and the country's level of corruption is quite low (Heritage 2012).
4. Australia has a more resilient tourist industry, with 75 % of tourism revenue coming from domestic sources. The recent strong Australian dollar has also prompted an increase in offshore tourism by 13 % (Taylor 2011).
5. Australia has demonstrated its ability to implement policies in an efficient and timely manner, which becomes a good model for coping with future external shock. For example, following the announcement of government stimulus in February 2009, the first set of projects was approved by April and construction was under way by June. This provided swift support for job creation in the labor-intensive construction industry and effectively mitigated the negative impact of the crisis (ILO 2010a).
6. Australia has benefited from commodity price increases since November 2011. Prices for coking and thermal coal have increased sharply, with the unusually cold weather in the Northern Hemisphere also contributing to the increase in

prices. This trend has provided Australia more leverage for future national development (RBA 2011).

7. The Australian government has included future growth planning in its stimulus packages, which aim to boost consumer protection, cut red tape for business, and deliver the government's commitment to modernize its economy (Treasurer 2009).
8. From January to August 2012, resource investment in Australia continued to expand rapidly. Work continued with the support of very large projects, capital imports grew strongly, and additional resource projects have commenced or gained approval (RBA 2012). These projects help accelerate Australia's recovery.

## *Canada*

Since exiting the recession in the third quarter of 2009, Canada's economy recorded positive growth for five consecutive quarters. According to the third quarter of the 2010 national accounts data, at the aggregate level, Canada's economy has recovered all the ground it lost during the recession (Chand 2011). This global recession has unveiled Canada's comparative strengths, including a sound estate market and a banking system that was recognized as the strongest in the world (Government of Canada 2012). The following prospects may explain a part of its future development.

1. Canada was ranked as the sixth freest economy in 2011 (Heritage 2012), which encourages investments and business activities.
2. Canada's immigrant population tends to be more highly skilled than that of the USA (Schuler 2011).
3. According to the IMF, Canada's stimulus plan is "large, timely, well diversified and structured for maximum effectiveness" (Government of Canada 2012), which facilitates a better recovery with good future prospect.
4. The Canadian economy has been the only industrialized nation to thrive during the difficult time of this financial crisis. The Toronto Dominion Bank was the 15th largest bank in North America in 2008; in 2012 it became the fifth largest. Now more than ever, Canada's financial system is the strongest in the world. In addition, Canadian households and businesses are in a much stronger financial position than most other industrialized countries after the financial crisis (Hansen 2012b).
5. The relatively small number of banks in Canada is seen as facilitating regulation and their domination of nationwide retail banking has shielded them from international competition. Although the consistent profitability of Canadian banks has been criticized as harmful to the interests of consumers, it also helped with bank resilience during the crisis (Porter 2010).
6. The Canadian government has introduced significant tax relief for Canadian businesses since 2006. The tax reductions in the Economic Action Plan further reinforce the Canadian government's ambitious agenda of tax relief aimed at

creating a tax system that improves standards of living, fuels job creation, and invests in Canadian businesses that are sustainable for the future. The plan was also designed to continuously support entrepreneurs and innovators as well as expand trade and focus on opening new markets for Canadian businesses (Government of Canada 2012).

7. With the support of the Economic Action Plan, Canada reached the goal of having the lowest overall tax rate on new business investment in the G7 in 2010. It also had the lowest statutory tax rate in the G7 in 2012. The competitiveness of the business tax system will encourage new investment in Canada, including direct investment from abroad. Provincial and territorial governments also reduce taxes, in line with the federal government, in recent years to boost business (Government of Canada 2012).
8. In 2012, a major priority of the plan included investing in worker training and infrastructure, expanding opportunities for aboriginal people to fully participate in the Canadian economy, and building a fast and flexible economic immigration system (Hansen 2012b).
9. Implementation of the Economic Action Plan has set a good model for the collaboration between the federal government and state governments. Approximately 40 % of the stimulus consists of the joint actions of federal, provincial, territorial, and municipal governments. In addition, to have the maximum impact on job creation during the crisis, the Canadian government moved aggressively to deliver budget spending up to 14 months faster than the usual process (Government of Canada 2012), which proved its capacity for efficient and effective policy implementation.
10. Canada has also participated in the G20-led global effort to make US$1 trillion in additional resources available to support emerging market economies experiencing financial crises and countries in need of continuous international trade (Government of Canada 2012).
11. Since 2006, the Canadian government has invested over US$1.9 billion (C$2.2 billion) in new science and technology measures. Its investments in higher education research and development (R&D) as a proportion of the economy are now the highest in the G7, and second in the OECD countries. Funding has been provided to support research excellence at Canadian post-secondary institutions, help Canadian scientists focus on areas where Canada can be world leaders, and then link such research strengths to the opportunities and challenges facing the private sector. Building on these measures, Canada's Economic Action Plan invests a further US$4.4 billion (C$5.1 billion) in science and technology initiatives, which is an unprecedented investment.
12. The Government is also investing in green infrastructure to improve the quality of the environment and create a more sustainable economy over the longer term, such as supporting a more dynamic and resilient integrated electrical power grid.

## *Japan*

Although Japan has been hit hard by this financial crisis, its private sector still has the capacity to purchase overseas properties during the most difficult time. The following characteristics may help explain the reasons and facilitate the country's future development.

1. During this financial crisis, Japanese businesses did a reasonably thorough cleaning of house, such as cutting costs and trimming workforces and idling factories (Hays 2011), which made them stronger in the wake of the crisis.
2. Despite the government's efforts to stimulate the economy, the Japanese have accumulated US$14 trillion in household savings from trade surpluses and frugal lifestyles (Wei 2009). Therefore, Japan did not face a financial meltdown like other Western countries. In other words, after financing its immense US$8.1 trillion fiscal deficit, Japan still has enough money left to be the world's largest creditor nation (Wei 2009).
3. Japan's five bank-bailout packages in the late 1990s provided critical lessons for this crisis. At that time, Japan spent nearly US$440 billion between 1998 and 2003 to assist and recapitalize its banking system, resulting in the emergence of today's sound financial system (Nanto 2008).
4. After the reforms, by 2008, Japanese banks and brokerage houses had become strong enough that Nomura Holdings had agreed to acquire the Europe and Middle East operations of Lehman Brothers as well as Lehman's franchise in Japan and Australia (Nanto 2008). In addition, healthy capital positions helped the Mitsubishi UFG Group, Japan's largest bank, buy 21% of Morgan Stanley for US$9 billion, giving them access to new markets and growth potential in the long run (Nanto 2009; Wei 2009). Mitsubishi UFG also laid out US$3.5 billion to buy the remaining 35% stake in Union Bank of California, giving it full ownership of the bank. Furthermore, Sumitomo Mitsui also injected several hundred billion yen into Goldman Sachs. Up to 25 September 2008, overseas acquisitions by Japanese banks and other financial institutions made up a total of US$12.5 billion (Wei 2009).
5. The Japanese government recognized the importance of pursuing economic growth through reform in the medium to long term for the next 10 years (Nanto 2009). As a result, a top priority of its reform has been on the labor market and the nonmanufacturing sector (OECD 2009). Reducing the number of national civil servants is also on the agenda (ILO 2010c).
6. Despite battling the crisis at home, in mid-November 2008, the Japanese government released up to US$100 billion to the IMF as financial aid to emerging economies and invested US$2 billion in a new World Bank fund to recapitalize banks in smaller emerging markets (Wei 2009).
7. Japan is also doing its part to insulate Southeast Asia as much as possible from the global financial crisis. Since October 13, 2008, Japan has reaffirmed that it would continue to invest in ASEAN countries (ASEAN, Association of Southeast Asian Nations) to make up for the slowdown in the USA and the EU as

much as possible (Wei 2009). Japan also initiated a cooperative venture known as the "East Asia Industrial Corridor" for ASEAN, China, South Korea, India, Australia, New Zealand, and Japan to invest in their logistics systems and create new shipping links (Wei 2009). This includes the New Delhi–Mumbai and the East–West Economic Corridor for ASEAN countries slated to be completed by 2025 (Wei 2009).

8. In addition to Japan's economic strength, the performance of Japanese students in the OECD's PISA assessment (PISA, Programme for International Student Assessment) is outstanding. In 2009, Japan ranked second among OECD countries in science, fourth in mathematics, and fifth in reading. In 2011, Japan's R&D spending is 3.4% of its gross domestic product (GDP), the fourth highest among the 34 OECD countries. The share of the adult population that has completed tertiary education in Japan is the second highest in the OECD area at 43% (Gurria 2011). Overall, Japan's strength in education and R&D gives the country a solid base on which to build a bright economic future (Gurria 2011).
9. The Japanese government also aims to create new demand and jobs in the fields of environment, health, and tourism, with the target of generating millions of jobs and US$1.1 trillion (¥100 trillion) in demand in these three sectors by 2020 (ILO 2010c). These endeavors are in line with Japan's New Growth Strategy, which focuses on green innovation, health care, economic integration with Asia, and regional development (OECD 2011b).
10. Although the March 2011 earthquake brought about devastating results, the experience of past disasters suggests that the negative short-term impact on economic output will be followed by a rebound as reconstruction spending picks up. The reconstruction spending is predicted to be more than US$70.2 billion (¥5.6 trillion) (1.1% of GDP) through the end of 2012. Such a pattern is projected to slow real GDP growth to 0.8% in 2011, followed by a pickup to 2.3% growth in 2012 (OECD 2011a). In addition, there have been signs of an acceleration in trade in the Asian region, which accounts for 56% of Japanese exports (OECD 2011a).
11. On the surface, Japan's problems of high debt–GDP ratio are the worst among those of the developed economies. However, unlike the USA and some European countries, Japan is still running a significant current account surplus, and close to 95% of its government debt is held by domestic investors (Iwaisako 2010). Therefore, Japan still had room to maneuver during the external shock.

## *New Zealand*

New Zealand was almost unaffected by the 2008 global financial crisis. The following prospects may help the country further its national development.

1. New Zealand was ranked the fourth freest economy in the 2011 (Heritage 2012). With a transparent and stable business climate, New Zealand has created a dyna-

mic entrepreneurial environment. The average tariff rate is low, and commercial operations are aided by a flexible labor market and efficient regulations (Heritage 2012).

2. New Zealand is the world's premier dairy exporter, demonstrating the efficiency of its agricultural sector under the complete absence of agricultural subsidies. The prices of dairy products are expected to rise in 2013 (The National Bank 2012). Therefore, New Zealand is in a good position to develop its future economy.
3. Tourism, which is primarily nature based, has been growing rapidly and has surpassed dairy as the nation's highest export earner (OECD 2011d).
4. New Zealand entered the crisis with a relatively strong fiscal position, based on a low public debt-to-GDP ratio. The country's precrisis decision on structural spending increases and tax cuts has provided a timely stimulus in 2009–2010 (OECD 2011d), which helps mitigate the external shock with a fast recovery for continuous growth.
5. The New Zealand government has set a target to keep its net debt below 40 % of its GDP and to return to around 30 % of its GDP no later than the early 2020s. Over the longer term, the government is shooting for its net debt to be closer to 20 % of its GDP. The government also aims to reduce its operating deficit from US$5.1 billion in 2010/2011 to US$2.7 billion in 2013/2014 (Treasury 2010).
6. New Zealand has led global efforts to measure and model agricultural emissions. The country is strict in turning Kyoto promises into policy actions with a goal to bring greenhouse gas (GHG) emissions back to the 1990 levels by 2012, even though the global crisis had intervened and uncertainties were high (OECD 2011d). The emission trading scheme is its major development and green growth would be a key advantage.
7. In New Zealand, there is a positive sentiment that the crisis will spur structural reforms and behavioral changes that can secure a stronger foundation for sustainable long-run growth. For example, government policy has been directed toward building up skill levels in the workforce and addressing skill shortages (Treasury 2010).
8. It is recognized that polices to pursue inclusive economic growth with sound environmental effects are essential to secure New Zealand's natural advantages in international competition (OECD 2011d).
9. For New Zealand, the Christchurch rebuild will be a key driver of its economic growth, with residential housing investment forecast to rise by 29 % in 2013 and a further 41 % in 2014 (McBeth 2012).

## *The United States*

The Geneva-based World Economic Forum said that the USA had several advantages, including highly sophisticated and innovative companies, an excellent university system, flexible labor markets, and its enormous domestic economy (Los Angeles Times 2011). Especially, one of the great advantages that the USA enjoys is that their best universities continue to attract the best talent in the world (Robertson n.d.).

To build a sustainable economy, green management has been particularly subsidized in the stimulus packages. Structural policies have been pursued through an extension of tax credit for renewable energy production (US$13.1 billion), funds were provided for investment in new energy transmission networks, and US$40 billion was allocated for investments in energy infrastructure (particularly the so-called smart grid technology).

In addition, financial support has focused on industries of the future; for example, besides supporting energy and environment sectors, US$25.1 billion was allocated to develop health information technology (Falke 2010).

To further create new jobs and improve the economy, the US government particularly emphasizes innovation. The government wants to expand the ability to quickly and efficiently transfer science and engineering breakthroughs from the laboratory to the commercial marketplace. As a result, Business USA, a one-stop, central online platform where small businesses and businesses of all sizes that want to begin or increase exporting, can access information about available federal programs without having to waste time navigating the federal bureaucracy (Quinn 2011).

Specifically, the platform directs agencies to streamline and accelerate the process for private–public research partnerships, small business R&D grants, and university start-up collaborations. It gives agencies more flexibility to partner with industries, encouraging them to create new partnerships with local communities, support the growth of regional innovation clusters, and share laboratory facilities with local businesses, among others. In addition, the platform will institute more accountability by directing agencies to develop a 5-year plan with concrete goals and metrics to measure progress, including keeping track of how many patents each laboratory is generating.

Furthermore, to facilitate this initiative, the United States Patent and Trademark Office (USPTO), in collaboration with the National Science Foundation (NSF), will pilot a program to provide Small Business Innovation Research (SBIR) awardees with comprehensive intellectual property support through the agency's small business programs and resources. The SBIR encourages domestic small businesses to engage in federal research, development, and commercialization through a competitive award-based program that enables small businesses to explore their technological potential and provides the incentive to profit from its commercialization (Quinn 2011).

As the USA continues to be the source of innovation in technology and management and entrepreneurship in industry (Robertson n.d.), with the additional government assistance, its results can be anticipated.

## Challenges

Alongside the prospects, there are challenges as well for these five advanced countries as briefly described hereunder.

### *Australia*

Although Australia has been ranked as one of the most attractive trade and investment destinations globally, its economy is not immune to global market conditions which are filled with uncertainty. Challenges the country faces may include the following:

1. The late 2010 floods indirectly impacted 10 % of businesses across Australia, with 37 % of business losses nationally not being covered by insurance, and in Queensland the rate was higher at 41 % (Taylor 2011). Although the influence is short term, it did accrue additional costs for the business added to the labor cost rise after the global financial crisis.
2. Australia's main economic challenges are medium term, including weakening productivity, boosting housing supply, widening the current account to finance mining investments, and ensuring noninflationary growth. Enhancing labor utilization in a socially inclusive manner is also an important aspect of promoting well-being in Australia (Kennedy 2009; OECD 2010).
3. Australia is a heavy commodity export country; its recent strong economic growth mainly relies on China's increasing demand. However, the World Bank warns that China's economy could slow down more quickly if Europe's sovereign debt crisis worsens (Glynn 2012). Such a result will indirectly impact Australia's economic health and deserves close attention with coping strategies. Such a warning is gradually realized as its energy industry has shed batch after batch of workers in the first part of 2013.
4. One 2012 McKinsey report (Taylor et al. 2012) warned Australia that, although resources investment surge has driven half of the country's growth during the recent 5 years (surpassed previous 20 years total), it also obscures the truth about its overall economic health. For example, the country has enjoyed 4.1 % annual gains in income since 2005, yet its growth in labor productivity has fallen to just 0.3 %. Capital productivity becomes the biggest drag on its income growth. Therefore, enhancing productivity, improving efficiency, implementing microeconomic reform, and creating a foundation for long-term competitiveness are crucial for Australia's sustainability.
5. Although Australia's tax burden is relatively low, the system includes numerous taxes with low yields and high administrative costs, which needs to be reconsidered for its effect. Some taxes and the complex transfer system can also dampen incentives to work and thereby weaken growth (OECD 2010).

6. With Australia's size, the geographical dispersion of its population and production centers, and its remoteness from other markets, adequate and well-functioning infrastructure will be essential for Australia's future growth and well-being (OECD 2010).
7. In addition to the pressure on infrastructure, Australia's long-term concerns also include aging of the population and environmental issues such as frequent droughts (CIA 2012).

## *Canada*

Even though Canada performed very well during this global financial crisis, the challenges it faces may include the following:

1. Canada has fallen out of the top ten rankings (ranked 12 in the Global Competitive Index (GCI) of 2011–2012) of global competitiveness as the country loses ground to fiercer Asian rivals (Schwab 2011). The country comes up short in terms of foreign direct investment. Trade tariffs, trade barriers, the foreign direct investment rules, and wasteful spending also hamper Canada's development.
2. Canada's productivity stagnation, income inequality, and resource over dependency have aroused some attention. Studies showed that Canadian businesses continue to underperform in using the skills and knowledge of human resources to generate new or improved products, processes, or services. In addition, critics also warned that Canadian businesses do not appear to be adapting adequately to globalization or building effective global value chains as quickly as their international competitors (Morrissy 2011).
3. The Canadian Economic Action Plan, together with the effects of the global recession, has resulted in a US$50.2 billion deficit for the 2012 fiscal year (Government of Canada 2012).
4. Future challenges for Canada also include overextended housing prices, recording a high household debt, a surging Canadian dollar, and a weak US economy. The latest figures from the Bank of Canada show that the total household debt reached US$1.43 trillion (C$1.47 trillion) in September 2010, up by 23 % from US$1.17 trillion (C$1.19 trillion) in December 2007. As a percentage of disposable income, Canadian household debt is at a record high of 148 % in early 2011. In general, to secure a stronger and more sustainable economy, Canada needs to rebalance its underlying structure of demand by moving more toward investment and exports and relying less on consumption that is being increasingly driven by debt (Chand 2011).
5. Canada faces the same aging labor force challenges as most of the developed Western countries do, combined with the extremely low population growth rate of 0.794 %. In 2010, 15.9 % of Canada's population was above the age of 65. The Conference Board of Canada predicts that after 2014 the labor market will again tighten as retirement rapidly increases and employers will consequently be forced to increase wages (Hansen 2012a).

## *Japan*

Japan's general challenges include the fact that its government debt is over 200 % of its GDP, as well as persistent deflation, reliance on exports to drive growth, and an aging and shrinking population (CIA 2012). The country's likely challenges can be categorized as financial management, international trade, labor market, education, business environment, manpower supply, health care and pension, and green management. The following summaries are mainly based on the suggestions of OECD (2009, 2011a, b), Heritage (2012), Gurria (2011), Jones (2011), and Jones and Urasawa (2011).

### Financial Management

1. Taxation in Japan is fairly burdensome, and its corporate tax rate is becoming increasingly uncompetitive.
2. A reform of the fiscal framework may help achieve the fiscal target, such as relying more on the consumption tax and the indirect taxes. The fiscal plan should be accompanied by social security reforms to limit spending pressures due to rapid population aging. Measures may also include environment-related levies to raise revenue, a stronger legal basis for the fiscal targets, and an objective fiscal body to monitor and evaluate the progress.
3. Spending on the 2011 earthquake and tsunami reconstruction has to be combined with efforts to improve the fiscal situation. In comparison with the 1995 Kobe earthquake, at that time, Japan's budget deficit and government debt were less than 5 and 86 % of its GDP, respectively; in 2011 they were around 9 and 200 %. Therefore, rebuilding is especially challenging this time.
4. Japan has to set its 2020 primary budget surplus at a level high enough, such as around 3 %, to ensure that it is sufficient to stabilize the ratio of gross government debt to GDP.
5. Japan may need to cut spending in government personnel costs and public investment in the medium term to offset rising social security outlays. In addition, continuation of the screening process to reduce low-priority and ineffective spending programs may also be required.

### International Trade

Although the export-oriented Japanese economy has long benefited from global trade, its nontariff barriers linger. Japan also lags behind other countries in pursuing bilateral trade agreements. At present, Japan has the lowest level of imports and inflows of FDI as a share of GDP and the lowest share of foreigners in the labor force in the OECD countries. Even though its New Growth Strategy has set an objective of doubling the inflow of people, goods, and capital by 2020, it still poses a great challenge to the country.

## Labor Market

1. Beginning in 2002, the labor productivity growth in Japan accelerated to more than 7 % per year in manufacturing, while remaining below 2 % in services. Since services account for 70 % of its value-added and employment, boosting productivity in the service sector is essential to sustain output growth and narrow the gap with the top OECD performers.
2. Labor market dualism is developing in Japan. To reduce the problem, a comprehensive approach that includes greater social insurance coverage of nonregular workers, better training programs, consultation on transition to regular employment, and preventing discrimination against nonregular workers is required. In addition, Japan can also work on encouraging greater use of flexible employment and wage systems to improve working conditions for older workers, in part by abolishing mandatory retirement at the age of 60.

## Education

1. In Japan, reforms to further raise the efficiency of educational spending per student (currently above the OECD average) are needed. Expanding the scope for school choice by students and parents can encourage schools to excel. At present, only 14 % of municipal school districts allow school choice. At the same time, the government should grant more autonomy for schools to excel.
2. The tertiary sector should be improved by strengthening competition through increased transparency about quality and by enhancing internationalization. Increasing transparency about the performance of students, such as labor market outcomes of graduates, should be encouraged. In addition, Japan can expand the vocational training role of universities and create vocational qualifications that are recognized by firms. Enhancing internationalization can be achieved through increasing the number of foreign students and encouraging the establishment of more foreign tertiary institutions in Japan.
3. The role of universities could be strengthened by enhancing labor mobility and cooperation of researchers between universities, firms, and government research institutes and raising the share of government R&D funding for universities, which is competitively financed.

### Business Environment

Japan can focus on accelerating regulatory reform to help create a more business-friendly environment to encourage private investments, business start-ups, and entrepreneurship. Reducing the cost of creating new firms, strengthening competition policy and innovation, and allowing local governments more autonomy with greater financial resources are ways to promote regional development, including the creation of innovation clusters.

### Manpower Supply

With the working-age population set to fall by almost 40 % by 2050, it is essential for Japan to fully utilize its human resources, including women and older persons. Female participation could be boosted by increasing the availability of child-care, thus promoting better work–life balance. In addition, the tax system should be reformed and the mandatory retirement age of 60 should be abolished to encourage better use of older workers.

### Health Care and Pension

With the population aging, health care and pension pose a great challenge for Japan. Promoting the shift of long-term care away from hospitals toward more appropriate institutions or home-based care may be required. The Japanese pension system is being reformed by raising the contribution rate to 18.3 % by 2017, allowing pension benefits to fall from around 60–50 %, and increasing the pension eligibility age gradually from 60 to 65 by 2025 for men and by 2030 for women. Nevertheless, smooth implementation of pension reform is a challenge.

### Green Management

Japan has targeted to reduce its GHG emissions 25 % by 2020 relative to 1990, yet it requires green innovation. A top priority is to establish a price on carbon, preferably through a mandatory and comprehensive cap-and-trade emission trading system (ETS), with the permits auctioned. Another measure would be an electricity certificate system, with incentives that decrease over time. Phasing out inefficient fossil fuel subsidies in line with the G20 initiative in order to ensure an appropriate price for carbon is also important.

## *New Zealand*

Although New Zealand has demonstrated its resilience during the financial crisis, risks remain including a combination of high external deficits and international debt, an overvalued exchange rate, a heavy cost of capital, and unbalanced growth (OECD 2011c). The challenges that New Zealand may face include the following:

1. After two waves of earthquakes, the total costs including business disruption or additional costs from inflation, insurance administration, and rebuilding with higher standards were around US$24 billion (NZ$30 billion) (Treasury 2012). The reconstruction poses opportunities as well as threats, which required aligned commitment from the relevant parties.
2. From the 2000s, New Zealand's main sources of rising prosperity increasingly became commodity-based term-of-trade improvements, credit-fueled capital gains on property, and rising government spending, rather than more enduring increases in productivity based on investment and production in the traded-goods sectors (OECD 2011d). In addition, its economic expansion was being held back by the strong exchange rate, falling commodity prices, the withdrawal of fiscal stimulus, and pressures for households to deleverage (OECD 2012b). What is more worrying is its long history of high current account deficits and large net external indebtedness (around 85 % of GDP), among the highest in the OECD (OECD 2011d).
3. New Zealand has not yet promoted the strengthening of regulations after this financial crisis. The relatively weak regulatory framework in the financial sector increases the vulnerability of many finance companies (Chiang and Prescott 2010). For example, the continued reliance on relatively short-term wholesale funding leaves the banks vulnerable to future shifts in investor sentiment (OECD 2011d).
4. Weak business investment and low national saving have for some time contributed to New Zealand's poor growth performance. The low national saving, persistently below the OECD average, impedes the deepening of financial markets and limits the country's ability to mobilize and allocate capital efficiently in the future (OECD 2011d). The country's generous universal public pension and student-loan schemes may reduce the incentive for households to save.
5. With the rapidly rising public debt and high external debt, New Zealand needs to adhere to its fiscal consolidation plans, in the form of spending restraint and tax and pension reforms to boost national saving (OECD 2011c). However, as the government shrinks, reinvigorated structural policies are needed to channel resources into productive economic uses (OECD 2012b). In addition, regulatory governance should also be further fortified to improve the overall investment environment. The government ownership of economic assets has increased, in contrast to OECD-wide trends. With the increase in state ownership, barriers to FDI have tightened (OECD 2011d). Therefore, moving toward full or even partial privatization of state-controlled commercial assets should be considered to strengthen market discipline and transparency (OECD 2011c).

6. There have been complaints about New Zealand's regulatory uncertainty resulting from sudden policy changes arising from too much ministerial discretion (OECD 2011d). The policy inconsistency may suppress entrepreneurship and investment.
7. According to the OECD (2011d), New Zealand's living standards have for some time tracked persistently below the OECD average, as well as Australia's. Despite robust terms-of-trade gains, a likely reason is poor labor productivity performance.
8. Even though New Zealand is committed to its Kyoto obligation, market-based instruments to give natural assets a value should be used more broadly, notably to allocate water efficiently (OECD 2011d). Therefore, more efficient water and land management should be a priority. Markets for water allocation and pollution rights, either formal or informal, should be encouraged by removing regional legal restrictions on trading (OECD 2011d).
9. Overall, the OECD recommends that New Zealand ease barriers to competition in network industries and to foreign direct investment, reduce regulatory opacity, reverse educational underachievement among the Maori and Pacific Islander populations, raise the effectiveness of public R&D support, and improve efficiency in the health-care sector and environmental policy (OECD 2011d).

## *The United States*

According to the US Central Intelligence Agency (CIA 2012), the long-term problems of the USA include inadequate investment in economic infrastructure, rapidly rising medical and pension costs of an aging population, sizable trade and budget deficits, and stagnation of family incomes in the lower economic groups. In addition, the USA may face the following challenges:

1. The US federal budget deficit is extremely large, with gross public debt approaching 100% of its GDP (Heritage 2012). The stimulus package, which was funded through normal budgetary channels, is estimated to have increased the federal debt by US$1 billion (Falke 2010). In addition, the merchandise trade deficit is very high—US$840 billion in 2008, US$507 billion in 2009, and US$647 billion in 2010 (CIA 2012). Although consolidation is necessary, it should be implemented at a steady, gradual pace consistent with a medium-term plan to restore fiscal stability (OECD 2012d).
2. Unemployment duration is still extremely high; about 40% of the unemployed have been out of work for 27 weeks or more (OECD 2012c). Policies to promote job creation and provide adequate training programs should be taken further.
3. The USA seems to be losing its economic edge, slipping to the fifth place in the Global Competitiveness Index (GCI) ranking, from number two in 2005 (Fig. 1.1). According to the World Economic Forum, the "lack of macroeconomic stability continues to be the United States' greatest area of weakness," pointing to murky policymaking, burdensome regulations, and wasteful alloca-

tions of resources. Effective regulations that provided greater transparency are needed (Los Angeles Times 2011).

4. In the longer term, education and training is the key to raising the skills and wages of the workforce (OECD 2012c) and the key to future American success. With the increasing importance of research and technology, students should be encouraged to see their graduate future in engineering rather than financial or legal services (Robertson n.d.).
5. To reduce both income inequality and distortions in resource allocation, tax expenditures that disproportionately benefit high earners should be limited over time. In particular, effective tax rates on debt-financed corporate investment and housing should be equalized at the higher rate on equity-financed corporate investment, while simultaneously lowering the corporate tax rate (OECD 2012c).
6. Social transfers could be more effective in alleviating poverty through better targeting of the truly needy and simplifying of transfer programs (OECD 2012c).
7. A proposed climate change bill that would have imposed federal constraints on energy use has been stalled (Heritage 2012).
8. The US economy faced more challenges in 2012 than the year before. The effects of the European recession and a slowdown in China weighed on US exports and industrial production in 2011 (Willis and Liu 2012). In 2013, the programmed expiration of tax cuts and emergency unemployment benefits, together with automatic federal spending cuts, will result in a sharp fiscal retrenchment that might derail the recovery (OECD 2012d).

## Policy Implications

In the wake of the 2008 global financial crisis, many potential causes for it have been suggested. The US Senate issued the Levin–Coburn Report (Levin and Coburn 2011) stating, “The crisis was not a natural disaster, but the result of high risk, complex financial products; undisclosed conflicts of interest; and the failure of regulators, the credit rating agencies, and the market itself to rein in the excesses of Wall Street.” Critics argued that credit-rating agencies and investors failed to accurately price the risk involved with mortgage-related financial products, and that governments did not adjust their regulatory practices to address twenty-first-century financial markets.

The above statements manifest that intangibles—people, systems, governance, market dynamics, and the global interdependence—are the key causes of this global financial catastrophe. National intellectual capital (NIC) represents a major part of national intangible assets. The research results reported in this booklet provide valuable information for policymakers to look back on the national intangibles before the crisis, observe their codevelopment with the GDP during and after the crisis, and then draw lessons from it.

By investigating economic development and NIC development from 2005 to 2010, we have been able to connect the co-evolution of tangibles and intangibles for the reported five advanced countries. The implications that can be drawn from our research findings are as follows.

*First, NIC development goes together with economic development and should be regarded as an enhancer of economic growth.* The codevelopment of NIC and GDP presented in Fig. 3.7 indicates that the higher the NIC, the higher the GDP per capita (ppp), based on the data of 48 countries. This means that intangible intellectual capital development accompanies GDP growth. In an era when knowledge and intangible assets become the key national driving force, the value of NIC deserves special attention, especially for advanced countries that rely more on value-added development.

*Second, the wisdom to strike a balance in the financial system between conservative and liberal, supervision and autonomy, and traditional practice and innovation is important.* In the wake of this global financial crisis, it becomes clear that countries weathered the crisis well, such as Australia and Canada, all adhering to prudent banking regulations. Before the crisis, they were often criticized as being too conservative, stagnant, and lacking in innovation. However, when things turned sour, their much criticized behaviors actually protected their countries from having a financial meltdown. On the contrary, countries responding to the requests for deregulation, more autonomy, less supervision, and relaxing risk control of innovative products such as sub-prime mortgage collapsed seriously in this crisis. Countries in this category include the epicenter of this crisis—the USA and Iceland which had the earliest financial collapse. Postcrisis financial practices will see more stringent regulations and supervision worldwide. However, over-rectification may stifle capital availability and business-friendly policies most needed after the crisis for speedier recovery. Therefore, establishing a balanced system requires the wisdom of key decision makers.

*Third, the effectiveness of stimulus packages will be judged by achieving national long-term goals rather than only the speed of recovery or reduction of the unemployment rate.* At the onset of this financial crisis, all the countries reported in this volume responded and put forth stimulus packages swiftly and timely, mainly from experiences gained from crises in the 1980s and 1990s. Some countries even provided several waves of packages, such as Australia and Japan. Unlike some countries in other regions, all countries reported in this volume wove their long-term goals into their stimulus packages. Examples include support for insulating the ceilings of existing homes in Australia, investments in green infrastructure in Canada, subsidies for replacing fuel-efficient cars in Japan, polices to pursue inclusive economic growth with sound environmental effects in New Zealand, and supporting energy and environment sectors in the USA. To upgrade the quality of human resources for future development, Australia guarantees a training place to all unemployed people aged 25 years and under in its stimulus package. To further create new jobs and improve the economy, the US government particularly emphasizes innovation and its ensuing commercialization. Compared with those of other country clusters, stimulus packages designed by these five advanced countries are more comprehensive and long-term oriented.

*Fourth, the soundness of national governance was tested in the global financial crisis which reflects the development of national intangible assets.* During this financial crisis, some countries have been able to mobilize their resources efficiently to soothe the urgent needs, yet some have internal dissonance. For example, following the announcement of the Australian government stimulus in February 2009, the first set of projects was approved by the month of April and construction was under way by June. In addition, to have the maximum impact on job creation during the crisis, the Canadian government moved aggressively to deliver budget spending up to 14 months faster than the usual process. In addition, in Canada and Japan, the federal or central government has successfully collaborated with local governments to accelerate the dispersion of stimulus packages for timely rescue. On the contrary, New Zealand experienced regulatory uncertainty resulting from sudden policy changes arising from too much ministerial discretion. In difficult times, internal dissonance may impede the speed of recovery and affect national well-being.

*Fifth, overdependence on single or limited sources of exports for growth will be unsustainable.* During this financial crisis, countries that relied heavily on the two major import regions, the USA and the EU, for international trade faltered. Those that extended their trade partners, especially to Asia, weathered the crisis better. That is, spreading the risk through diversification should be an effective resilience-building measure. With the principle, Australia and New Zealand exit the crisis less impaired due to its increasing trade with China. However, their overdependence on commodity export presents a potential risk. Similarly, Canada's heavy reliance on the US market is also risk-bound. Countries reported in this volume have large-enough domestic markets, except New Zealand. To build a more resilient economy, longer-term national development strategies concerning the degree of both internal and external diversification need to be carefully pondered.

*Sixth, in addition to monitoring government debt, household debt and its cause should also be reviewed for national health.* During this financial crisis, the government debt percentage of the GDP is an important indicator to examine the economic health of a country. However, this report reveals that household debt is also an indicator of gauging the soundness of an economy. For example, persistent low household savings in New Zealand has weakened the capacity of their banks to respond to external shock. Studies showed that low interest rates and generous student loans have reduced the need for New Zealand households to save and encourage lending. Such good policies with negative side effects should be reconsidered. On the contrary, Japan has an extremely high government debt, approaching 200 % of its GDP. Nevertheless, their private sector is rich and strong enough to purchase partial shares of Lehman Brothers, Goldman Sachs, and 21 % of Morgan Stanley. In addition, the Japanese have an accumulated US$14 trillion in household savings, which is sufficient enough that the country does not have to worry about a financial meltdown.

*Seventh, advanced countries need to help increase global public good in addition to private good, especially in difficult times.* During this global financial crisis,

**Table 5.1** Similarities and differences of Australia and Canada

| | GDP per capita (ppp) | | | Government debt 2012 (est.) # | GCI 2005/2010/2012 | NIC/ change | Strong NIC |
|---|---|---|---|---|---|---|---|
| | 2005–2010 average | 2011 # | 2012 (est.) # | | | | |
| Australia | US$37,204 | US$39,699 | US$41,468 | 24% | 10/20/20 | 13/down | PC |
| Canada | US$37,770 | US$39,057 | US$41,335 | 84.7% | 14/12/12 | 12/up | HC |

#from Global Finance online data, *GCI* Global Competitiveness Index ranking, *PC* process capital, *HC* human capital

no country was immune from credit crunch and capital dry-up. These five advanced countries were no exception. However, in difficult times, countries that still stretch their hands to those that are even more desperate are especially worthy of respect. For example, Canada is one of the countries that participated in the G20-led global effort to make US$1 trillion in additional resources available to support emerging market economies experiencing financial crises. Japan is another country that released up to US$100 billion to the IMF as financial aid to emerging economies and invested US$2 billion in a new World Bank fund to recapitalize banks in smaller emerging markets. Furthermore, in late 2008, Japan reaffirmed that it would continue to invest in ASEAN countries to make up for the slowdown in the USA and the EU and help stabilize the economy in that region. These countries live up to their roles as advanced countries that promote global well-being.

*Eighth, advanced countries should set the model of environmentally friendly economic development for developing countries to follow.* After the financial crisis, three of the five countries reported in this volume encountered serious natural disasters. Australia experienced floods in late 2010, Japan encountered a devastating earthquake followed by a tsunami in March 2011, and New Zealand had two waves of earthquake in September 2010 and February 2011, respectively. These disasters slowed down their economic recoveries. Global climate change may partially explain the increasing seriousness of natural disasters. Advanced countries should be more aggressive in framing an environment-friendly economic development model, especially those that were victimized.

*Ninth, observing the national development of Australia and Canada in the immediate future may provide significant implications.* From most of the graphs presented in Chap. 3, developments in Australia and Canada were either intertwined or not far apart from each other. Their GDP per capita (ppp) growth is extremely similar as shown in Table 5.1, yet their intangibles are quite different. The GCI of Australia declined from number 10 in the world in 2005 to 20 in 2010 and 2012, whereas that of Canada advanced from number 14 in 2005 to 12 in 2010 and 2012. Their average NIC ranking over 2005–2010 is similar, number 13 versus 12. However, year-by-year NIC scores (Fig. 3.6) and NIC ranking changes over the three time periods (Table 3.2) indicate that the NIC of Australia is going down, whereas that of Canada is going up. In addition, Australia is relatively strong in process capital (short-term NIC) and Canada is better in human capital (long-term NIC). Like running a race, with a similar starting point (GDP per capita ppp) and different intangibles, it will be insightful to follow up on their national development in the next 5–10 years to see how each country ends up.

*Tenth, unbalanced NIC development may jeopardize future economic development.* The most intriguing finding in this report is that Japan outperformed New Zealand in almost every indicator; however, the distance of Japan to the targeted GDP of Norway is farther than that of New Zealand. Further examination reveals that among the five deficiency factors (Table 3.4) in Japan, two are government-related issues (process capital) and two are market capital-related issues. The deficiency factors are the results of comparing all indicators of a particular country with those of the benchmarking country, Norway. Ranking comparisons (Appendix 6) between Japan and Norway indicate 34 versus 14 and 18 versus 7 for market capital and process capital, respectively. The same comparisons between New Zealand and Norway show rankings of 15 versus 14 and 16 versus 7, respectively; that is, the disparity between Japan and Norway is wider than that between New Zealand and Norway, which might be the reason why the route to the target is farther for Japan than New Zealand. For these five advanced countries, only Japan's market capital is in the middle capability region. This finding implies that Japan's serious lag in market capital development may hamper a balanced economic development in the future.

## Concluding Remarks and Emerging Insights

In retrospect, according to the US federal inquiry, the 2008 financial crisis was an *avoidable* disaster caused by widespread failures in government regulations, corporate mismanagement, and heedless risk-taking by Wall Street (Chan 2011). In addition, corporate leaders and directors might not have fully understood the risks of the securities in which they were investing (Lo 2009). Such man-made negligence has incurred huge tangible and intangible costs.

For the past several decades, the global economy has experienced many difficulties, including the savings and loan crisis and stock market crash of 1987; the junk bond market collapse in 1989; the currency-related crises in Latin America in 1994 and Asia in 1997; the bursting of the dot-com bubble in 2001; the economic effects of 9/11; the near-global financial meltdown triggered by the Lehman collapse in 2008; and then the European sovereign debt crisis (Bedell 2012). Every crisis poses threats as well as opportunities. Countries that are able to learn lessons, even though in a hard way, will become more and more resilient, as in the cases of Australia, Canada, and Japan.

With these prior experiences, fortunately a great recession was avoided due to national and international measures that prevented the 2008 global financial crisis from deteriorating. Advanced countries such as those reported in this volume played an important role in helping to bring the global economy back to order, mainly for their better knowledge, systems, resources, and experience. The very origin of the financial crisis—people, systems, governance, market dynamics, and the global interdependence—is also the key to the economic recovery in any place and country.

As a recap, to counter the worsening economic conditions worldwide, a total of US$2 trillion in stimulus packages, amounting to approximately 3 % of the world GDP, were allocated (some of the packages include measures that extend into subsequent years), an amount that exceeds the call by the IMF for fiscal stimulus totaling 2 % of the global GDP. The IMF also reported that, as of January 2009, the US fiscal stimulus packages as a percentage of the GDP in 2009 would amount to 1.9 %, for the Euro area 0.9 %, for Japan 1.4 %, for Asia excluding Japan 1.5 %, and for the rest of the G20 countries 1.1 % (Nanto 2009). In the coming years of 2013 and 2014, the world economy may remain in a three-speed mode. Emerging markets are still growing rapidly, the US recovery is steady, but much of Europe continues to struggle (TJT 2013).

Furthermore, there will be a rise in the intangible economy. In July 2013, the US Bureau of Economic Analysis announced that R&D will no longer be treated as a mere expense; it will be categorized in the government's books as an investment (Coy 2013). Original works of art such as films, music, and books will also be treated for the first time as long-lived assets. This change brings the national accounts more closely in line with the way the economy works in the USA. In the knowledge economy, the economic landscape has become quite different from what it was decades ago. For example, nine out of the ten most valuable companies in the world have their headquarters in the USA; however, only three—General Electric, ExxonMobil, and Chevron—are in the world's top ten for tangible fixed capital (Coy 2013). In other words, the US economy is very much NIC driven, and so are many advanced economies.

In terms of future NIC development, our other study of the top ten NIC ranking countries reveals that the interplay among the four capitals—human capital, market capital, process capital, and renewal capital—resulted in the best synergic prospect for GDP growth. When their weaker capital (process capital) interacts with stronger capital (market capital), both effects on the GDP are enhanced (Lin 2011). Such a finding agrees with the shortfall of Japan's unbalanced intangible capital development, especially in market capital.

It is a fundamental function of the government to create and maintain both tangible and intangible infrastructures under which the economic, social, and cultural lives of the citizens can prosper. Looking back at the 2008 global financial crisis through the lens of NIC provides a different perspective for the policymakers to ponder on.

At the completion of this reporting, we have a strong understanding that national success is a capability that can be accumulated meticulously over time; it is not a free gift nor can it be achieved from overnight wealth. National economic development is built upon the well-coordinated tangible and intangible systems, including human capital, market capital, process capital, and renewal capital systems described in this booklet. As it takes time to develop the intangibles, countries that are determined to enhance their so-called soft power need to consider the added-value issue from the start of their policymaking.

# Appendices

**Appendix 1** Summary of the main stimulus packages of the five advanced countries

| Country | Date | Amount | Item |
|---|---|---|---|
| Australia | Oct. 14, 2008 | #1 #2<br>US$7.3 billion (Australian $ 10.4 billion) | Cash payments to pensioners and low and middle income earners. Single pensioners received US$ 987 (Australian $ 1400), while pensioners who are part of a couple received US$ 1,480 (Australian $ 2100) |
| | | | US$ 2.7 billion (Australian $ 3.9 billion) for low and middle income families received a one-time payment of US$ 705 (Australian $ 1000) for each child in their care |
| | | | US$ 1.1 billion (Australian $ 1.5 billion) to help Australians buy their first home. Double the grant for first-time home buyers from US$ 4,933 (Australian $ 7,000) to US$ 9,865 (Australian $ 14,000). An extra US$ 9,865 (Australian $ 14,000) for first home buyers who buy a newly constructed house, taking their home buyers grant to US$ 14,798 (Australian $ 21,000) |

C. Y.-Y. Lin et al., *National Intellectual Capital and the Financial Crisis in Australia, Canada, Japan, New Zealand, and the United States*, SpringerBriefs in Economics,
DOI 10.1007/978-1-4614-9308-2, © The Author(s) 2014

| Country | Date | Amount | Item |
|---|---|---|---|
| | Dec. 12, 2008 | #3, #4<br>US$ 3.1 billion (Australian $ 4.7 billion) | US$ 3.1 billion (Australian $ 4.7 billion) infrastructure spending to boost growth and create 32,000 jobs<br>Additional US$ 3.1 billion (Australian $ 4.7 billion) for rail road and education projects. US$ 788 million (Australian $ 1.2 billion) for Australian Rail Track Corporation and US$ 1.1 billion (Australian $ 1.6 billion) for university infrastructure<br>US$ 1 billion (Australian $ 1.5 billion) for 2008–2009 and US$ 1.8 billion (Australian $ 2.7 billion) for 2009–2010 spending<br>A 10 % temporary investment allowance for small businesses to spur capital investment and a 20 % cut in the next quarterly pay-as-you-go tax installment |
| | Feb. 3, 2009 | #5<br>US$ 26 billion (Australian $ 42 billion) | The massive stimulus package was aimed at national building and supporting up to 90,000 jobs<br>Cash handouts of US$ 8.2 billion (Australian $ 12.7 billion) to eligible workers, farmers, and students<br>Up to US$ 615 (Australian $ 950) would be paid to workers earning US$ 64,726 (Australian $ 100,000) or less, supporting up to 8.7 million individuals |
| | May 2009 | #6, #7<br>Stimulus program as 4.6 % of 2008 GDP<br>US$ 9.3 billion (Australian $ 9.7 billion, 0.82 % of 2008 GDP)<br>US$ 2.2 billion (Australian $ 2.9 billion, 0.25 % of 2008 GDP)<br>US$ 11.8–12.8 billion (Australian $ 15.7–17 billion, up to 1.4 % of 2008 GDP)<br>US$ 4.3 billion (Australian $ 5.7 billion, 0.48 % of 2008 GDP) | Infrastructure<br>Science, R&D, and innovation<br>Education<br>Green technology |

| Country | Date | Amount | Item |
|---|---|---|---|
| Canada | Since 2008 | #8 | US$ 5.2 billion (Canadian $ 5.3 billion) in Employment Insurance to support the unemployed<br>US$ 2.9 billion (Canadian $ 3 billion) was given over 2 years for postsecondary education and jobs in research, technology, and innovation.<br>Another US$ 2.9 billion (Canadian $ 3 billion) was provided for creating and protecting jobs in the communities and industries most affected by the recession, including the forestry, agriculture, and manufacturing sectors |
| | Jan. 27, 2009 | #9 #10<br>US$ 32 billion (Canadian $ 40 billion) | Spending of US$ 32 billion (Canadian $ 40 billion) over five years to create190,000 jobs by 2011<br>Tax cuts for lower and middle-income earners worth US$ 16.3 billion (Canadian $ 20 billion)<br>US$ 9.8 billion (Canadian $ 12 billion) in infrastructure spending including roads, bridges, and clean energy programs over 2 years<br>US$ 1.5 billion (Canadian $ 1.9 billion) in tax measures for businesses<br>Targeted loans and worker training<br>Around US$ 10.4 billion (Canadian $ 13 billion), budgeted by Export Development Canada and the Business Development Bank of Canada were available to lend to Canadian businesses<br>Around US$ 9.6 billion (Canadian $ 12 billion), supported by Canadian Secured Credit Facility for leasing cars and equipment |
| | May 2009 | #6, #7 Stimulus program as 4.1 % of 2008 GDP<br>US$ 17.3 billion (Canadian $ 20.3 billion, 1.27 % of 2008 GDP)<br>US$ 680 million (Canadian $ 800 million, 0.05 % of 2008 GDP)<br>US$ 1.6 billion (Canadian $ 1.9 billion, 0.12 % of 2008 GDP)<br>US$ 2.4 billion (Canadian $ 2.8 billion, 0.18 % of 2008 GDP) | Infrastructure<br>Science, R&D and innovation<br>Education<br>Green technology |

| Country | Date | Amount | Item |
|---|---|---|---|
| Japan | Aug. 29, 2008 | #11 US$ 18.4 billion (¥2 trillion) | Supports for nonregular workers, employment security in SMEs, women, the elderly, and people with disabilities |
| | Oct. 30, 2008 | #11 US$ 51.3 billion (¥5 trillion) | Supports for families in care of the disabled and childcare services<br>Strengthen employment safety nets<br>US$ 3.1 billion (¥300 billion) for employment-related measures and US$ 2.6 billion (¥250 billion) for employment creation to meet the special needs of local communities |
| | Dec. 19, 2008 | #11 US$ 111.7 billion (¥10 trillion) | Supports for housing and daily living expenses, employment security and reemployment, reinforcement of the employment insurance system, and employment offers by companies<br>About US$ 23.5 billion (¥2.1 trillion) were for employment-related elements, such as setting up the Emergency Job Creation Program US$ 1.7 billion (¥150 billion) |
| | Apr. 10, 2009 | #11 US$ 153.5 billion (¥15.4 trillion) | About US$ 18.9 billion (¥1.9 trillion) for employment-related measures, including supports for foreign workers. US$ 3 billion (¥300 billion) was added to the Emergency Job Creation Program<br>Established "The Second Safety Net," with a budget of US$ 7 billion (¥700 billion) for those who are not covered by unemployment insurance |
| | Aug. 29, 2009 | #11 US$ 21.4 billion (¥2 trillion) | Supports for nonregular workers, employment security in SMEs, employment for women, the elderly, and the disables, and ensuring long-term care services |
| | Oct. 23, 2009 | #11 | Emergency support for workers and new graduates<br>Established an emergency job creation program in three sectors—care services, green industry, and local social enterprises |
| | Dec. 8, 2009 | #11 US$ 81 billion (¥7.2 trillion) | US$ 6.8 billion (¥600 billion) for employment-related measures, including strengthening support for the poor and new graduates, expanding emergency job creation programs, and enhancing childcare to facilitate female employment |

| Country | Date | Amount | Item |
|---|---|---|---|
| | Sep. 10, 2010 | #12<br>US$ 10.9 billion (¥915 billion) around 0.2 % of the GDP | The US$ 10.9 billion (¥915 billion) for incentives and reforms to help employment, consumer spending and corporate investment |
| | Nov. 26, 2010 | #13<br>US$ 61 billion | To create jobs through measures to help small businesses and boost consumer spending |
| New Zealand | Nov. 26, 2008 | #14<br>US$ 3.8 billion (New Zealand $ 7 billion) around 4 % of GDP | US$ 3.8 billion (New Zealand $ 7 billion) to boost the economy over 2 years |
| | Feb. 4, 2009 | #15<br>US$ 260 million (New Zealand $ 500 million) | For 69 new state houses and renovations of 10,000 more, five new schools and five major state highway developments |
| | 2008–2010 | #6<br>US$ 5,404 million | Fiscal packages |
| The USA | Feb. 7, 2008 passed<br>Feb. 13, 2008 signed | #16<br>US$ 152 billion | US$ 300 for every individual who falls under specified income limit<br>Business tax incentives were provided to commercial establishments as a one-time payment and depreciation tax deduction |
| | Feb. 17, 2009<br>Sep. 30, 2009 | #17<br>US $ 787 billion | Tax cuts for individuals and business, 33.3 %<br>Aid to states for health care and other essentials, 14.4 %<br>Education, 14.2 %<br>Aid for the unemployed and the needy, 12.9 %<br>Infrastructure, 10.9 %<br>Energy investments, 6.6 %<br>Investment in science and technology, 1.9 %<br>Other spending, 5.8 %<br>Many of the components contain "green" investments, which comprise 12 % of the total stimulus spending<br>A US $ 25 supplement to the weekly benefit allowance paid by states to eligible unemployed recipients through December 31, 2009<br>US $ 300 million for Supplemental Nutrition Assistance Program (SNAP) administrative expenses in fiscal years 2009 and 2010.<br>US $ 60 billion for training American workers for green jobs and emerging industries<br>US$ 82.5 billion in aid to strengthen social protection and improve employment prospects |

| Country | Date | Amount | Item |
|---|---|---|---|
| | May 2009 | #6, #7 US$ 804,070 million Stimulus program as 5.6 % of 2008 GDP<br>US$ 100 billion, 0.7 % of 2008 GDP<br>US$ 16 billion, 0.11 % of 2008 GDP<br>US$ 83 billion, 0.58 % of 2008 GDP<br>US$ 59 billion, 0.41 of 2008 GDP | Fiscal packages<br>Infrastructure<br>Science, R&D and innovation<br>Education<br>Green technology |
| | Dec.17, 2009 | #17 US$ 154 billion | For Jobs Bill |


1. The New York Times. (October 14, 2008). Australia plans $ 7.3 billion stimulus package. Retrieved from http://www.nytimes.com/2008/10/14/business/worldbusiness/14iht-14ozecon.16925314.html
2. Australianpolitics.com. (October 14, 2008). Rudd announces $ 10.4 billion economic stimulus package. Retrieved from http://australianpolitics.com/2008/10/14/rudd-announces-104-billion-economic-stimulus-package.html
3. Pannett, R. (December 12, 2008). Kevin Rudd unveils $ 4.7 billion infrastructure boost. *The Australian.* Retrieved from http://www.theaustralian.com.au/business/breaking-news/rudd-in-47bn-infrastructure-boost/story-e6frg90f-1111118299352
4. Nanto, D.K. (October 2, 2009). Global Financial Crisis: Analysis and Policy Implications. Congressional Research Service. Retrieved from http://www.fas.org/sgp/crs/misc/RL34742.pdf
5. AFP. (February 2, 2009). Australia launches massive stimulus package. Retrieved from http://www.google.com/hostednews/afp/article/ALeqM5hboUVK4spDjFCc-7GRk2652rXQjQ
6. OECD. (June, 2009). *Policy Responses to the Economic Crisis: Investing in innovation for long-term growth.* Retrieved from http://www.oecd.org/dataoecd/59/45/42983414.pdf
7. Breuss, F., Kaniovski, S., & Schratzenstaller, M. (2009). Macro-economic Effects of the Fiscal Stimulus Measures in Austria. *Austrian Economic Quarterly* (14.4) 205–216. Retrieved from http://fritz.breuss.wifo.ac.at/Breuss_Kaniovski_Schratzenstaller_Macro-economic_Effects_Fiscal_Stimulus_Austria_AEQ_4_2009.PDF
8. Hansen, D. (May 8, 2012) Moving to Canada: Canada's economic action plan, Canadianimmigrant.ca. Retrieved from http://canadianimmigrant.ca/guides/moving-to-canada/canadas-economic-action-plan
9. BBC. (January 28, 2009). Canada unveils stimulus package. Retrieved from http://news.bbc.co.uk/2/hi/7855311.stm
10. The Star.com (January 27, 2009) Stimulus package worth $ 35B. Retrieved from http://www.thestar.com/news/canada/federalbudget/article/578084–stimulus-package-worth-35b

11. International Labor Office (ILO) (April, 2010a) G20 Country Briefs—Japan's response to the crisis. Meeting of Labor and Employment Ministers. Retrieved from http://www.dol.gov/ilab/media/events/G20_ministersmeeting/G20-japan-brief.pdf
12. Turner, S. (September 10, 2010). Japan unveils $ 10.9 billion stimulus package. *Market Watch*. Retrieved from http://articles.marketwatch.com/2010–09-10/markets/30726707_1_stimulus-package-gdp-data-japanese-cabinet-office
13. BBC. (November 26, 2010). Japan passes new $ 61 billion stimulus package. Retrieved from http://www.bbc.co.uk/news/business-11844483
14. NZPA. (November 26, 2008). Stimulus package to inject $ 7 billion into NZ economy. *The National Business Review*. Retrieved from http://www.nbr.co.nz/article/stimulus-package-inject-7-billion-nz-economy-38313
15. Monsters and Critics. (February 10, 2009). New Zealand government announces stimulus package. Retrieved from http://news.monstersandcritics.com/business/news/article_1458746.php/New_Zealand_government_announces_stimulus_package
16. Economy Watch. (June 30, 2010). About US economic stimulus. Retrieved from http://www.economywatch.com/economic-stimulus/world-economic-stimulus/usa.html
17. International Labor Office (ILO) (April, 2010b) G20 Country Briefs—The United States' response to the crisis. Meeting of Labor and Employment Ministers. Retrieved from http://www.dol.gov/ilab/media/events/G20_ministers-meeting/G20-us-brief.pdf

**Appendix 2** Important meetings held by world leaders to address the 2008 global financial crisis

| Date | Place | Participants |
|---|---|---|
| June 18–19, 2012 | Los Cabos, Mexico | G20 |
| June 17, 2012 | Los Cabos, Mexico | G7 finance ministers |
| March 1–2, 2012 | Brussels | European Council |
| January 30, 2012 | Brussels | Informal meeting of members of the European Council |
| December 8–9, 2011 | Brussels | European Council |
| November 12–13, 2011 | Honolulu, USA | 19th APEC Economic Leaders' Meeting |
| November 3–4, 2011 | Cannes, France | G20 |
| October 23, 2011 | Brussels | European Council |
| September 10, 2011 | Marseille | G8 Deauville Partnership finance ministers |
| September 9–10, 2011 | Marseille | G7 finance ministers and central bank governors |
| July 21, 2011 | Brussels | Meeting of heads of state or government of the Euro area |
| June 23–24, 2011 | Brussels | European Council |
| March 24–25, 2011 | Brussels | European Council |

| Date | Place | Participants |
|---|---|---|
| March 17, 2011 | Japan | G7 finance ministers telephone conference |
| March 11, 2011 | Brussels | extraordinary European Council |
| February 4, 2011 | Brussels | European Council |
| December 16–17, 2010 | Brussels | European Council |
| November 21, 2010 | Ireland | G7 finance ministers |
| November 13–14, 2010 | Yokohama, Japan | 18th APEC Economic Leaders' Meeting |
| November 11–12, 2010 | Seoul, Korea | G20 |
| October 28–29, 2010 | Brussels | European Council |
| October 8, 2010 | Washington DC | G7 finance ministers and central bank governors |
| September 16, 2010 | Brussels | European Council |
| June 26–27, 2010 | Toronto, Canada | G20 |
| June 17, 2010 | Brussels | European Council |
| March 25–26, 2010 | Brussels | European Council |
| February 11, 2010 | Brussels | Informal meeting of heads of state or government of the European Union |
| February 5–6, 2010 | Iqaluit, Nunavut, Canada | G7 finance ministers and central bank governors |
| December 10–11, 2009 | Brussels | European Council |
| November 19, 2009 | Brussels | Informal meeting of heads of state or government of the European Union |
| November 14–15, 2009 | Singapore | 17th APEC Economic Leaders' Meeting |
| October 29–30, 2009 | Brussels | European Council |
| October 3, 2009 | Istanbul, Turkey | G7 finance ministers and central bank governors |
| September 24–25, 2009 | Pittsburgh, USA | G20 |
| September 17, 2009 | Brussels | Informal meeting of heads of state or government of the European Union |
| June 18–19, 2009 | Brussels | European Council |
| June 12–13, 2009 | Lecce, Italy | G8 finance ministers |
| April 24, 2009 | Washington DC | G7 finance ministers and central bank governors |
| April 2, 2009 | G20 London Summit, United Kingdom | G20 |
| March 19–20, 2009 | Brussels | European Council |
| February 2009 | Rome | G7 finance ministers and central bank governors |
| December 11–12, 2008 | Brussels | European Council |
| November 2008 | Peru | G20 APEC |
| November 22–23, 2008 | Lima, Peru | 16th APEC Economic Leaders' Meeting |
| November 14–15, 2008 | Washington D.C., USA | G7 |
| October 15–16, 2008 | Brussels | European Council |
| October 10, 2008 | Washington, DC | G7 Finance Ministers |
| September 1, 2008 | Brussels | Extraordinary European Council |
| July 7–9, 2008 | Tokyo, Japan | 34th G8 Summit |

| Date | Place | Participants |
|---|---|---|
| June 19–20, 2008 | Brussels | European Council |
| June 13–14, 2008 | Osaka | G8 Finance Ministers Meeting |
| March 13–14, 2008 | Brussels | European Council |
| February 9, 2008 | Tokyo | G7 Finance Ministers and Central Bank Governors Meeting |

For further information:

http://g20mexico.org/en/g20/previous-leaders-summits
http://www.g8.utoronto.ca/finance/index.htm
http://video.consilium.europa.eu/ecofin/
http://www.european-council.europa.eu/council-meetings/conclusions
http://www.apec.org/

## **Appendix 3** Indicators in each type of capital

| | |
|---|---|
| *Human capital index* | *Market capital index* |
| Skilled labor* | Corporate tax* |
| Employee training* | Cross-border venture* |
| Literacy rate | Openness of culture* |
| Higher education enrollment | Globalization* |
| Pupil-teacher ratio | Transparency* |
| Internet subscribers | Image of country* |
| Public expenditure on education | Exports of goods |
| *Process capital index* | *Renewal capital index* |
| Business competition environment* | Business R&D spending |
| Government efficiency* | Basic research* |
| Intellectual property rights protection* | R&D spending/GDP |
| Capital availability* | R&D researchers |
| Computers in use per capita | Cooperation between universities and enterprises* |
| Convenience of establishing new firms* | Scientific articles |
| Mobile phone subscribers | Patents per capita (USPTO + EPO) |

Financial capital is the logarithm of GDP per capita adjusted by purchasing power parity
Indicators with objective numbers are transformed to scores between 1–10 by calculating the ratio to the highest number in that indicator and then multiplying by 10
Readers can refer to the book *National Intellectual Capital: A Comparison of 40 Countries* for model validation details (www.nic40.org)
*Rated qualitatively using a scale of 1–10

## **Appendix 4** Definition of the 29 indicators

| Indicators | Definition |
|---|---|
| *Human capital* | |
| Skilled labor* | Whether skilled labor is readily available |
| Employee training* | Whether employee training is a high propriety in companies |
| Literacy rate | Adult (over 15 years) literacy rate as a percentage of population |

| Indicators | Definition |
| --- | --- |
| Higher education enrollment | Percentage of population that has attained at least tertiary education |
| Pupil–teacher ratio | Ratio of teaching staff to students |
| Internet subscribers | Number of internet users per 1000 people |
| Public expenditure on education | Total public expenditure on education (percentage of GDP) |
| *Market capital* | |
| Corporate tax encouragement* | Whether corporate taxes encourage entrepreneurial activity |
| Cross-border venture* | Whether international transactions can be freely negotiated with foreign partners |
| Openness to foreign culture* | Whether the national culture is open to foreign culture ideas |
| Attitudes toward globalization* | Whether attitudes toward globalization are generally positive in a given society |
| Transparency* | Whether transparency of government policy is satisfactory |
| Country image* | Whether the image abroad of a given country encourages business development |
| Exports of goods | Exports of goods (Percentage of GDP) |
| *Process capital* | |
| Business competition environment* | Whether competition legislation is efficient in preventing unfair competition |
| Government efficiency* | Whether government bureaucracy hinders business activity |
| Intellectual property rights protection* | Whether intellectual property rights are adequately enforced |
| Capital availability* | Whether cost of capital encourages business development |
| Computers in use per capita | Number of computers per 1000 people |
| Convenience of establishing new firms* | Whether creation of firms is supported by legislation |
| Mobile phone subscribers | Number of subscribers per 1000 inhabitants |
| *Renewal capital* | |
| Business R&D spending | Business expenditure on R&D (per capita) |
| Basic research* | Whether basic research enhances long-term economic development |
| R&D spending/GDP | Total expenditure on R&D (percentage of GDP) |
| R&D researchers | Total R&D personnel nationwide per capita (Full-time work equivalent per 1000 people) |
| Cooperation between universities and enterprises* | Whether knowledge transfer is highly developed between universities and companies |
| Scientific articles | Scientific articles published by origin of author (per capita) |
| Patents per capita (USPTO + EPO) | USPTO and EPO total patents granted (per capita) |
| *Financial Capital* | |
| GDP per capita (PPP) (From IMF) | Gross domestic product based on purchasing-power-parity (PPP) per capita |

## **Appendix 5** 48 countries by cluster and by continent

This booklet series covers a total of 48 countries in 11 country clusters. China, Brazil, and South Africa are grouped twice to maintain cluster completeness. China is in both Greater China region and BRICKS region, Brazil is in both BRICKS region and Latin American region, and South Africa is in both BRICKS region and in Cluster 5.

### Eleven country clusters:

1. Portugal, Italy, Greece, Spain
2. Greater China region (China, Hong Kong, Singapore, Taiwan)
3. Brazil, Russia, India, China, Korea, South Africa (BRICKS)
4. Indonesia, Malaysia, the Philippines, Thailand
5. Israel, Jordan, Turkey, South Africa
6. Bulgaria, Czech Republic, Hungary, Romania, Poland
7. Austria, Belgium, the Netherlands, Switzerland
8. France, Germany, Ireland, United Kingdom
9. Argentina, Brazil, Chile, Colombia, Mexico, Venezuela
10. Australia, Canada, Japan, New Zealand, USA
11. Denmark, Finland, Iceland, Norway, Sweden

### Forty-eight countries by continent:

**Europe—24 countries**

| | |
|---|---|
| Nordic Europe | Denmark, Finland, Iceland, Norway, and Sweden |
| Western Europe | Austria, Belgium, France, Germany, Ireland, the Netherlands, Switzerland, and United Kingdom. |
| Southern Europe | Greece, Italy, Portugal, and Spain |
| Eastern Europe | Russia |
| East Central Europe | Bulgaria, Czech Republic, Hungary, Poland, Romania, and Turkey |

**Americas—8 countries**

| | |
|---|---|
| North America | Canada and the USA |
| Latin America | Argentina, Brazil, Chile, Colombia, Mexico, and Venezuela |

**Australia—2 countries**

Australia and New Zealand

**Asia—13 countries**

| | |
|---|---|
| East Asia | China, Hong Kong, Japan, Korea, and Taiwan |
| West Asia | Israel and Jordan |
| Southeast Asia | Indonesia, Malaysia, Philippines, Singapore, and Thailand |
| South Asia | India |

**Africa—1 country**

South Africa

**Appendix 6** National intellectual capital (NIC) scores and ranking for 48 countries (2005–2010)

| 2005–2010 | Human capital | | Market capital | | Process capital | | Renewal capital | | Financial capital | | NIC | |
|---|---|---|---|---|---|---|---|---|---|---|---|---|
| Mean | 6.420 | | 5.409 | | 5.345 | | 3.658 | | 9.115 | | 29.946 | |
| SD | 1.217 | | 1.085 | | 1.454 | | 2.056 | | 0.690 | | 5.840 | |
| Country | Score | Ranking | Score | Ranking | Score | Ranking | Score | Ranking | Score | Ranking | Score | Ranking |
| Argentina | 5.370 | 36 | 3.340 | 47 | 3.038 | 47 | 1.413 | 45 | 8.755 | 34 | 21.916 | 45 |
| *Australia* | *7.205* | *15* | *6.199* | *12* | *6.938* | *9* | *4.927* | *16* | *9.695* | *11* | *34.964* | *13* |
| Austria | 7.229 | 14 | 6.203 | 11 | 6.982 | 8 | 5.296 | 12 | 9.708 | 10 | 35.418 | 11 |
| Belgium | 7.666 | 8 | 5.519 | 23 | 5.924 | 21 | 4.706 | 17 | 9.635 | 14 | 33.450 | 19 |
| Brazil | 4.757 | 44 | 4.589 | 38 | 3.076 | 46 | 1.753 | 36 | 8.481 | 40 | 22.656 | 42 |
| Bulgaria | 5.493 | 34 | 4.929 | 31 | 4.054 | 36 | 1.589 | 41 | 8.646 | 37 | 24.710 | 35 |
| *Canada* | *7.855* | *6* | *6.137* | *13* | *6.464* | *15* | *5.064* | *14* | *9.710* | *9* | *35.229* | *12* |
| Chile | 5.414 | 35 | 6.663 | 5 | 5.163 | 28 | 1.710 | 37 | 8.784 | 32 | 27.734 | 30 |
| China | 4.942 | 39 | 5.184 | 28 | 3.746 | 40 | 2.099 | 33 | 7.967 | 44 | 23.938 | 40 |
| Colombia | 4.941 | 40 | 4.677 | 36 | 3.951 | 37 | 1.435 | 44 | 8.348 | 42 | 23.352 | 41 |
| Czech Republic | 5.995 | 30 | 5.720 | 18 | 5.378 | 25 | 2.905 | 24 | 9.271 | 27 | 29.269 | 25 |
| Denmark | 8.545 | 1 | 6.662 | 6 | 7.642 | 1 | 6.587 | 6 | 9.665 | 13 | 39.101 | 3 |
| Finland | 7.601 | 9 | 6.232 | 10 | 7.399 | 3 | 7.755 | 3 | 9.606 | 17 | 38.593 | 4 |
| France | 6.956 | 20 | 4.141 | 45 | 5.730 | 22 | 4.500 | 20 | 9.585 | 18 | 30.912 | 23 |
| Germany | 6.761 | 23 | 5.630 | 19 | 6.489 | 14 | 5.796 | 9 | 9.612 | 16 | 34.287 | 17 |
| Greece | 5.986 | 31 | 4.216 | 43 | 4.113 | 35 | 2.168 | 32 | 9.440 | 23 | 25.923 | 31 |
| Hong Kong | 6.564 | 25 | 8.090 | 2 | 7.209 | 5 | 3.277 | 23 | 9.794 | 4 | 34.934 | 14 |
| Hungary | 6.674 | 24 | 4.836 | 32 | 5.095 | 29 | 2.301 | 29 | 9.046 | 29 | 27.952 | 29 |
| Iceland | 8.357 | 3 | 5.614 | 21 | 6.561 | 12 | 5.931 | 8 | 9.713 | 8 | 36.154 | 8 |
| India | 3.926 | 48 | 5.620 | 20 | 3.556 | 42 | 1.954 | 34 | 7.285 | 48 | 22.340 | 44 |
| Indonesia | 4.062 | 47 | 4.832 | 33 | 3.257 | 44 | 1.519 | 42 | 7.594 | 46 | 21.263 | 47 |
| Ireland | 7.145 | 16 | 6.816 | 3 | 6.711 | 11 | 4.101 | 21 | 9.768 | 5 | 34.541 | 16 |
| Israel | 8.040 | 4 | 5.954 | 16 | 6.454 | 17 | 7.091 | 4 | 9.414 | 24 | 36.953 | 6 |
| Italy | 6.471 | 28 | 4.155 | 44 | 5.184 | 27 | 2.745 | 26 | 9.479 | 22 | 28.035 | 28 |
| *Japan* | *7.581* | *10* | *4.820* | *34* | *6.209* | *18* | *6.473* | *7* | *9.576* | *19* | *34.659* | *15* |
| Jordan | 5.345 | 37 | 5.341 | 26 | 4.411 | 32 | 2.212 | 30 | 7.865 | 45 | 25.174 | 33 |
| Korea | 6.964 | 19 | 5.123 | 29 | 5.282 | 26 | 4.595 | 19 | 9.383 | 25 | 31.348 | 22 |
| Malaysia | 6.538 | 26 | 6.410 | 9 | 5.567 | 23 | 2.186 | 31 | 8.740 | 35 | 29.442 | 24 |
| Mexico | 4.871 | 42 | 4.491 | 39 | 3.226 | 45 | 1.237 | 48 | 8.781 | 33 | 22.606 | 43 |
| The Netherlands | 7.312 | 12 | 6.761 | 4 | 6.879 | 10 | 5.163 | 13 | 9.739 | 7 | 35.855 | 10 |
| *New Zealand* | *7.123* | *18* | *5.999* | *15* | *6.460* | *16* | *3.701* | *22* | *9.380* | *26* | *32.662* | *21* |
| Norway | 7.936 | 5 | 6.055 | 14 | 7.008 | 7 | 4.961 | 15 | 9.987 | 1 | 35.947 | 9 |
| Philippines | 4.772 | 43 | 4.464 | 40 | 3.317 | 43 | 1.268 | 47 | 7.481 | 47 | 21.302 | 46 |
| Poland | 6.393 | 29 | 4.246 | 41 | 3.895 | 38 | 1.819 | 35 | 8.945 | 30 | 25.299 | 32 |
| Portugal | 6.882 | 22 | 4.801 | 35 | 5.470 | 24 | 2.467 | 27 | 9.224 | 28 | 28.844 | 26 |
| Romania | 5.829 | 32 | 4.219 | 42 | 3.806 | 39 | 1.685 | 38 | 8.594 | 39 | 24.133 | 39 |
| Russia | 5.530 | 33 | 3.860 | 46 | 3.588 | 41 | 2.349 | 28 | 8.822 | 31 | 24.150 | 38 |
| Singapore | 7.144 | 17 | 8.306 | 1 | 7.506 | 2 | 5.416 | 11 | 9.961 | 2 | 38.334 | 5 |
| South Africa | 4.708 | 45 | 4.976 | 30 | 4.472 | 31 | 1.677 | 39 | 8.472 | 41 | 24.306 | 37 |
| Spain | 6.524 | 27 | 4.649 | 37 | 5.033 | 30 | 2.787 | 25 | 9.484 | 21 | 28.476 | 27 |

| 2005–2010 | Human capital | | Market capital | | Process capital | | Renewal capital | | Financial capital | | NIC | |
|---|---|---|---|---|---|---|---|---|---|---|---|---|
| Mean | 6.420 | | 5.409 | | 5.345 | | 3.658 | | 9.115 | | 29.946 | |
| SD | 1.217 | | 1.085 | | 1.454 | | 2.056 | | 0.690 | | 5.840 | |
| Country | Score | Ranking | Score | Ranking | Score | Ranking | Score | Ranking | Score | Ranking | Score | Ranking |
| Sweden | 8.385 | 2 | 6.563 | 7 | 7.174 | 6 | 7.780 | 2 | 9.673 | 12 | 39.575 | 1 |
| Switzerland | 7.575 | 11 | 6.481 | 8 | 7.374 | 4 | 7.988 | 1 | 9.753 | 6 | 39.172 | 2 |
| Taiwan | 7.244 | 13 | 5.823 | 17 | 6.026 | 20 | 5.425 | 10 | 9.526 | 20 | 34.044 | 18 |
| Thailand | 5.310 | 38 | 5.524 | 22 | 4.365 | 33 | 1.436 | 43 | 8.304 | 43 | 24.938 | 34 |
| Turkey | 4.703 | 46 | 5.227 | 27 | 4.167 | 34 | 1.666 | 40 | 8.690 | 36 | 24.453 | 36 |
| United Kingdom | 6.939 | 21 | 5.440 | 24 | 6.090 | 19 | 4.697 | 18 | 9.626 | 15 | 32.793 | 20 |
| *The USA* | *7.695* | *7* | *5.348* | *25* | *6.558* | *13* | *6.715* | *5* | *9.886* | *3* | *36.202* | *7* |
| Venezuela | 4.884 | 41 | 2.761 | 48 | 2.545 | 48 | 1.277 | 46 | 8.625 | 38 | 20.092 | 48 |

## **Appendix 7** Country profile—additional statistics

### 1. International reserves in millions of US$

| Country | 2005 | 2006 | 2007 | 2008 | 2009 | 2010 |
|---|---|---|---|---|---|---|
| Australia | 35,275 | 42,835 | 55,806 | 30,965 | 30,179 | 34,852 |
| Canada | 36,199 | 35,966 | 39,231 | 42,950 | 43,423 | 56,544 |
| Japan | 827,200 | 837,712 | 892,677 | 992,620 | 996,002 | 1,015,271 |
| New Zealand | 6,255 | 9,078 | 14,537 | 19,471 | 11,543 | 16,660 |
| USA | 67,901 | 54,311 | 55,510 | 64,723 | 63,916 | 1166,480 |

Source: Global Finance http://www.gfmNICag.com/

### 2. GDP per capita (PPP) Current international dollar

| Country | 2005 | 2006 | 2007 | 2008 | 2009 | 2010 |
|---|---|---|---|---|---|---|
| Australia | 33,862 | 35,310 | 37,321 | 38,282 | 38,751 | 39,699 |
| Canada | 35,150 | 36,943 | 38,454 | 39,046 | 37,971 | 39,057 |
| Japan | 30,315 | 31,943 | 33,657 | 34,009 | 32,199 | 33,805 |
| New Zealand | 24,938 | 25,693 | 26,919 | 27,206 | 26,600 | 26,966 |
| USA | 42,681 | 44,823 | 46,577 | 47,155 | 45,934 | 47,284 |

Source: World Economic Outlook Database http://www.imf.org/external/ns/cs.aspx?id=28

### 3. GDP (PPP)—share of world total %

| Country | 2005 | 2006 | 2007 | 2008 | 2009 | 2010 |
|---|---|---|---|---|---|---|
| Australia | 1.23 | 1.20 | 1.19 | 1.19 | 1.22 | 1.19 |
| Canada | 2.00 | 1.95 | 1.90 | 1.86 | 1.83 | 1.79 |
| Japan | 6.83 | 6.63 | 6.44 | 6.21 | 5.87 | 5.81 |
| New Zealand | 0.18 | 0.18 | 0.17 | 0.17 | 0.17 | 0.16 |
| USA | 22.26 | 21.74 | 21.04 | 20.43 | 19.90 | 19.53 |

Source: World Economic Outlook Database http://www.imf.org/external/ns/cs.aspx?id=28

4. Gross domestic expenditure on R&D as a % of GDP

| Country | 2005 | 2006 | 2007 | 2008 | 2009 | 2010 |
|---|---|---|---|---|---|---|
| Australia | 1.69 | 1.82 | 1.84 | 2.09 | 2.07 | 2.24 |
| Canada | 1.9 | 1.98 | 1.96 | 1.89 | 1.84 | 1.95 |
| Japan | 3.2 | 3.17 | 3.32 | 3.4 | 3.44 | 3.45 |
| New Zealand | 1.22 | 1.15 | 1.18 | 1.18 | 1.22 | 1.2 |
| USA | 2.66 | 2.67 | 2.61 | 2.67 | 2.76 | 2.77 |

Source: IMD World Competitiveness Yearbook 2006–2011

5. Household saving rates percent of disposable household income

| Country | 2005 | 2006 | 2007 | 2008 | 2009 | 2010 |
|---|---|---|---|---|---|---|
| Australia | −0.1 | 2.1 | 3.2 | 5.5 | 9.8 | 9.3 |
| Canada | 2.1 | 3.5 | 2.8 | 3.9 | 4.6 | 4.8 |
| Japan | 3.9 | 3.8 | 2.4 | 2.2 | 5.0 | 6.2 |
| New Zealand | −8.3 | −8.9 | −4.0 | −4.5 | −2.2 | 0.2 |
| USA | 1.5 | 2.6 | 2.4 | 5.4 | 5.1 | 5.3 |

Source: Global Finance http://www.gfmag.com/

# Glossary

| | |
|---|---|
| ARRA | American Recovery and Reinvestment Act |
| Basel II | Basel II is the second of the Basel Accords, which are recommendations on banking laws and regulations issued by the Basel Committee on Banking Supervision. Basel II, initially published in June 2004, was intended to create an international standard for banking regulators to control how much capital banks need to put aside to guard against the types of financial and operational risks banks face. |
| BBC | British Broadcasting Corporation |
| CIA | The USA Central Intelligence Agency |
| COBRA | Consolidated Omnibus Budget Reconciliation Act in the USA |
| CPI | Consumer price inflation |
| ETS | Emission trading system |
| EU | European Union |
| FC | Financial capital |
| FDI | Foreign direct investment |
| Fed | Federal Reserve in the USA |
| GCI | GCI Global Competitiveness Index (published by World Economic Forum) |
| GDP | Gross domestic product |
| GDP per capita (PPP) | Gross domestic product per capita adjusted by purchasing power parity |
| GHG emission | Greenhouse gas emission |
| HC | Human capital |
| IMPP | Insured Mortgage Purchase Program in Canada |
| IMD | International Institute for Management Development |
| IMF | International Monetary Fund |
| London FTSE | The FTSE 100 Index, also called FTSE 100, is a share index of the 100 companies listed on the London Stock Exchange with the highest market capitalization. It is one of the most widely used stock indices and is seen as a gauge of business prosperity for business regulated by UK company law. |

C. Y.-Y. Lin et al., *National Intellectual Capital and the Financial Crisis in Australia, Canada, Japan, New Zealand, and the United States*, SpringerBriefs in Economics, DOI 10.1007/978-1-4614-9308-2, © The Author(s) 2014

| | |
|---|---|
| Long-term NIC | Long-term oriented national intellectual capital, represented by human capital and renewal capital |
| MBS | Mortgage-backed securities in the USA |
| MC | Market capital |
| NIC | National intellectual capital |
| NSF | National Science Foundation in the USA |
| OECD | Organization for Economic Cooperation and Development |
| OSFI | Office of the Superintendent of Financial Institutions Canada |
| PC | Process capital |
| PPP | Purchasing power parity |
| R&D | Research and development |
| RC | Renewal capital |
| SBIR | Small Business Innovation Research in the USA |
| SD | Standard Deviation |
| Short-term NIC | Short-term oriented national intellectual capital, represented by market capital and process capital |
| SMEs | Small and Medium-Sized Enterprises |
| SNAP | Supplemental Nutrition Assistance Program, formerly Food Stamps in the USA |
| TARP | Troubled Asset Relief Program in the USA |
| Three time periods | For the convenience of comparing ranking changes, the 6 years data were separated into three time periods, namely 2005–2006, 2007–2008, and 2009–2010. Two years each represents "before, during, and after" the 2008 global financial crisis. Even though Euro zone is still in sovereign debt trouble as of mid-2012, the time partition is based on the financial crisis progression in the epicenter. The signs of financial trouble appeared in 2007 and the crisis was declared over in the third quarter of 2009. |
| USPTO | The United States Patent and Trademark Office |

# References

Access Economics. (2008, November). The impact of the global financial crisis on social services in Australia, prepared for Anglicare Australia, Catholic Social Services Australia, The Salvation Army and Uniting Care Australia. http://www.anglicare.org.au/news-research-events/latest-research/the-impact-of-the-global-financial-crisis-on-social-services-in-australia.

BBC. (2009, January 28). Canada unveils stimulus package, BBC News. http://news.bbc.co.uk/2/hi/7855311.stm.

Bedell, D. (2012). Resilience under pressure, Words of wisdom: Gerald Hassell, Bank of New York Mellon. In F. Andrea (Ed.), *Global finance: looking back, moving forward.* http://www.gfmag.com/archives/155–25th-anniversary/11807-words-of-wisdom-resilience-under-pressure.html#axzz23q600LdT.

Bergevin, P. (2008, December). The global financial crisis and its impact on Canada, International Affairs, Trade and Finance Division. http://www.parl.gc.ca/Content/LOP/researchpublications/prb0834_05-e.htm.

Bryant, L. (2011, September 8). Growth expected to slow in world's largest economies, Voice of America News. http://www.voanews.com/english/news/europe/OECD– Economic-Slowdown-Likely-to-Continue-129458543.html.

Central Intelligence Agency (CIA). (2012). The world factbook, U.S.A. Central Intelligence Agency. https://www.cia.gov/library/publications/the-world-factbook/index.html.

Chan, S. (2011, January 25). Financial crisis was avoidable, inquiry finds, The New York Times. http://www.nytimes.com/2011/01/26/business/economy/26inquiry.html?_r=2 & scp=1 & sq=financial%20crisis%20was%20avoidable,%20inquiry%20finds & st=cse.

Chand, R. (January, 2011). Canada's economy faces challenges, International economist & financial author. http://rangachand.com/commentary/2011/01/canadas-economy-faces-challenges/.

Chiang, C., & Prescott, S. (2010). The financial crisis in New Zealand: An inconvenient truth, Faculty of Business, AUT university. http://w3.manukau.ac.nz/aaac/ARA_2010_papers/Chiang_Prescott.pdf

Chossudovsky, M. (2009, January 25). Canada's 75 billion dollar bank bailout, Global Research Canada, Center for Research on Globalization. http://www.globalresearch.ca/index.php?context=va & aid=12007

Colvin, G. (February, 2013). The case for optimism: How this year could be lucky '13, Bank of American Merrill Lynch, originally published in the 2.4.13 issue of Fortune. http://corp.bankofamerica.com/business/bi/perspective/resource?p_a_id=647046 & g_id=10157 & cm_mmc=GCB-Integrated-_-MSN-PS-_-2013%20economic%20outlook-_-Feb.%202013%20-%20Lucky%2013%20Article%20-%20Phrase. Accessed 14 July 2013.

Coy, P. (July 18, 2013). The rise of the intangible economy: U.S. GDP counts R & D, artistic creation, Bloomberg Business Week. http://www.businessweek.com/articles/2013-07-18/the-rise-of-the-intangible-economy-u-dot-s-dot-gdp-counts-r-and-d-artistic-creation.

C. Y.-Y. Lin et al., *National Intellectual Capital and the Financial Crisis in Australia, Canada, Japan, New Zealand, and the United States*, SpringerBriefs in Economics, DOI 10.1007/978-1-4614-9308-2, 

Debelle, G. (March 31, (2009). Some effects of the global financial crisis on Australian financial markets, Finance Professionals Forum. http://www.rba.gov.au/speeches/2009/sp-ag-310309.html.

Department of Finance Canada. (2011). Canada's economic action plan – A seventh report to Canadians, Chapter 1 Overview, Department of Finance Canada. http://www.fin.gc.ca/pub/report-rapport/2011-7/ceap-paec-1-eng.asp.

Dow Jones Business News (DJBN). (July 11, 2013). Rudd says boom over as unemployment nears financial crisis levels, Nasdaq, Dow Jones Business News. http://www.nasdaq.com/article/rudd-says-boom-over-as-unemployment-nears-financial-crisis-levels-20130711-00043. Accessed 14 July 2013

Durocher, B. P. (October 14, 2008). The impact of the financial crisis in Canada, Economic Viewpoint, Desjardins Economic Studies. http://www.desjardins.com/en/a_propos/etudes_economiques/actualites/point_vue_economique/pve81014.pdf.

Edvinsson, L., & Malone, M. S. (1997). *Intellectual Capital: Realizing your company's true value by finding its hidden brainpower*. New York: Harper Business.

Falke, A. (2010). USA Country Report. In: Bertelsmann Stiftung (ed.), *Managing the Crisis. A Comparative Assessment of Economic Governance in 14 Economies*. Gütersloh: Bertelsmann Stiftung, 2010. http://www.bertelsmann-transformation-index.de/pdf/USA.pdf.

Global Finance. (2013a). Country report. http://www.gfmag.com/.

Global Finance. (2013b). World's GDP growth by region, Global Finance. http://www.gfmag.com/component/content/article/119-economic-data/12376-economic-dataworlds-gdp-growth-by-regionhtml.html#axzz2Z8YBShkn. Accessed 15 July 2013.

Glynn, J. (May 23, (2012). Growth robust but challenges ahead, new data reports show, The Australian Business with the Wall Street Journal. http://www.theaustralian.com.au/business/economics/economic-growth-still-below-par-westpac-report/story-e6frg926–1226364318836.

Government of Canada. (2012). Canada's economic action plan: Overview. Government of Canada. http://actionplan.gc.ca/eng/feature.asp?pageId = 116.

Gurria, A. (2011). Japan will bounce back quickly from the great east earthquake, OECD. http://www.oecd.org/document/52/0,3746,en_21571361_44315115_47694900_1_1_1_1,00.html.

Hansen, D. (May 8, 2012a). Moving to Canada: How the economy weathered the financial crisis, Canadian Immigrant. http://canadianimmigrant.ca/guides/moving-to-canada/moving-to-canada-how-the-economy-weathered-the-financial-crisis.

Hansen, D. (May 8, 2012b). Moving to Canada: Canada's economic action plan, Canadian Immigrant. http://canadianimmigrant.ca/guides/moving-to-canada/canadas-economic-action-plan.

Hays, J. (October, 2011). Japan, the global economic crisis in 2008 and afterwards: Hard times, stimulus and slight recovery, Facts and Details. http://factsanddetails.com/japan.php?itemid=1100&catid=24&subcatid=155.

Hepker, C. (June 25, 2010). G20: Why we all want to be Canadian now, BBC Business News. http://www.bbc.co.uk/news/10409354.

Heritage Foundation. (2012). Economic freedom. http://www.heritage.org.

International Monetary Fund. (January 24, 2012). World economic outlook update: Global recovery stalls, downside risks intensify. International Monetary Fund. http://www.imf.org/external/pubs/ft/weo/2012/update/01/.

International Labor Office (ILO). (April, 2010a). G20 Country Briefs – Australia's response to the crisis. Meeting of Labor and Employment Ministers. http://www.dol.gov/ilab/media/events/G20_ministersmeeting/G20-australia-brief.pdf.

International Labor Office (ILO). (April, 2010b). G20 Country briefs—Canada's response to the crisis. Meeting of Labor and Employment Ministers. http://www.dol.gov/ilab/media/events/G20_ministersmeeting/G20-canada-brief.pdf.

International Labor Office (ILO). (April, 2010c). G20 Country Briefs – Japan's response to the crisis. Meeting of Labor and Employment Ministers. http://www.dol.gov/ilab/media/events/G20_ministersmeeting/G20-japan-brief.pdf.

International Labor Office (ILO). (April, 2010d). G20 country briefs—United States' response to the crisis. Meeting of Labor and Employment Ministers. http://www.dol.gov/ilab/media/events/G20_ministersmeeting/G20-us-brief.pdf.

International Monetary Fund (IMF). (April, 2013). World economic outlook: Hopes, realities, and risks. Chapter 1: Global prospects and policies. http://www.imf.org/external/pubs/ft/weo/2013/01/pdf/c1.pdf. Accessed 14 July 2013.

Iwaisako, T. (2010). Japanese macroeconomic policy management after the global financial crisis, Policy Research Institute, Ministry of Finance, Japan. *Public Policy Review, 6*(5), 795–806. http://www.mof.go.jp/english/pri/publication/pp_review/ppr011/ppr011b.pdf.

Jones, R. S. (September 6, 2011). Education reform in Japan, OECD *Economics Department Working Papers*, No. 888. doi:10.1787/5kg58z7g95np-en. http://www.oecd-ilibrary.org/economics/education-reform-in-japan_5kg58z7g95np-en.

Jones, R. S., & Tsutsumi, M. (2009). Financial stability: Overcoming the crisis and improving the efficiency of the banking sector in Japan, OECD *Economics Department Working Papers*, No. 738. http://www.oecd.org/officialdocuments/displaydocumentpdf/?cote=eco/wkp(2009)79&doclanguage=en.

Jones, R. S., & Urasawa, S. (September 6, 2011). Labor market reforms in Japan to improve growth the equity, OECD *Economics Department Working Papers*, No. 889. doi:10.1787/5kg58z6p1v9q-en. http://www.oecd-ilibrary.org/economics/labour-market-reforms-in-japan-to-improve-growth-and-equity_5kg58z6p1v9q-en.

Kennedy, S. (June 24, 2009). Australia's response to the global financial crisis, A speech to the Australia Israel Leadership Forum. http://www.treasury.gov.au/documents/1576/HTML/docshell.asp?URL=Australia_Israel_Leadership_Forum_by_Steven_Kennedy.htm.

Kehoe, T. (2010). The current financial crisis in Spain: What should we learn from the great depressions of the twentieth century? University of Minnesota and Federal Reserve Bank of Minneapolis, 18th Barcelona Lecture, Barcelona G.S.E. and Banc Sabadell, February 2010.

Kuroda, H. (January 26, 2012). Asia to power world economy in 2012: ADB chief, The Economic Times. http://economictimes.indiatimes.com/news/economy/foreign-trade/articlelist/1200949414.cms.

Levin, C., & Coburn, T. (April 13, 2011). Wall Street and the financial crisis: Anatomy of a financial collapse, United States Senate. http://www.levin.senate.gov/imo/media/doc/supporting/2011/PSI_WallStreetCrisis_041311.pdf.

Lin, C. Y. Y. (2011). Leveraging intellectual capital for future competitiveness in Finland, Presentation at Tekes, Helsinki on November 10, 2011.

Lin, C. Y. Y., & Edvinsson, L. (2011). *National Intellectual Capital: A comparison of 40 countries*. NY: Springer Publishing Co.

Lo, A. W. (2009). Regulatory reform in the wake of the financial crisis of 2007–2008. *Journal of Financial Economic Policy, 1*(1), 4.

Los Angeles Times. (September 7, 2011). U.S. global economic competitiveness trails Sweden, Finland, Business – Los Angeles Times. http://latimesblogs.latimes.com/money_co/2011/09/us-global-economic-competitiveness-trails-sweden-finland.html.

Lynch, K. (2010). Avoiding the financial crisis: Lessons from Canada, Options Politiques. http://www.irpp.org/po/archive/may10/lynch.pdf.

McBeth, P. (May 24, 2012). Budget 2012: NZ economic outlook deteriorates on Chch rebuild delays, global instability, the National Business Review.

Menon, N. (July 9, 2013). IMF raises Canada 2013 growth view to 1.7 %, cuts 2014 view, Nasdaq, Dow Jones Business News. http://www.nasdaq.com/article/imf-raises-canada-2013-growth-view-to-17-cuts-2014-view-20130709-00549. Accessed 14 July 2013.

Michelis, A. (2009). Overcoming the financial crisis in the United States, Economics Department Working Paper No. 669, OECD. http://www.oecd.org/officialdocuments/displaydocumentpdf/?cote=eco/wkp(2009)10&doclanguage=en.

Morrissy, J. (September 7, 2011). Canada falls out of top 10 most competitive economies. http://www.vancouversun.com/business/Canada+falls+most+competitive+economies/5364462/story.html.

Nadeau, J. F. (March 13, 2009). The insured mortgage purchase program, Parliament of Canada, International Affairs, Trade and Finance Division. http://www.parl.gc.ca/Content/LOP/ResearchPublications/prb0856-e.htm.

Nanto, D. K. (2008). The U.S. financial crisis: Lessons from Japan, CRS report for Congress Order Code RS22960. http://fpc.state.gov/documents/organization/110816.pdf.

Nanto, D. K. (2009). The global financial crisis: Analysis and policy implications, CRS Report for Congress, Congressional Research Service 7-5700, RL34742, October 2, 2009.

OECD. (2009). Economic survey of Japan 2009: Overcoming the global crisis, the need for a new growth model, OECD. http://www.oecd.org/document/19/0,3746,en_2649_34111_43783443_1_1_1_1,00.html.

OECD. (2010). OECD economic surveys: Australia, November 2010 overview, OECD. http://www.oecd.org/economy/economicsurveysandcountrysurveillance/46467368.pdf.

OECD. (2011a). Japan's economic outlook following the 11 March 2011 earthquake, OECD. http://www.oecd.org/document/25/0,3746,en_2649_34569_47675097_1_1_1_1,00.html.

OECD. (2011b). OECD economic surveys Japan April 2011 overview, OECD. http://www.oecd.org/fr/economie/etudeseconomiquesparpays/47651425.pdf.

OECD. (2011c). Economic survey of New Zealand 2011, OECD. http://www.oecd.org/document/34/0,3746,en_2649_33733_47611554_1_1_1_1,00.html.

OECD. (2011d). OECD economic surveys New Zealand April 2011 overview, OECD.

OECD. (2011e). United States—Economic forecast summary, OECD. http://www.oecd.org/document/48/0,3746,en_2649_34573_45268528_1_1_1_1,00.html.

OECD. (2012a). Canada—Economic forecast summary (May 2012), OECD. http://www.oecd.org/document/55/0,3746,en_2649_34109_45268663_1_1_1_1,00.html.

OECD. (2012b). New Zealand—Economic forecast summary (May 2012), OECD. http://www.oecd.org/document/46/0,3746,en_2649_34109_45270062_1_1_1_1,00.html.

OECD. (2012c). Economic survey of the United States 2012, OECD. http://www.oecd.org/document/32/0,3746,en_2649_33733_50634144_1_1_1_1,00.html.

OECD. (2012d). United States—Economic forecast summary (May 2012), OECD. http://www.oecd.org/document/48/0,3746,en_2649_34109_45268528_1_1_1_1,00.html.

Porter, T. (2010). Canadian banks in the financial and economic crisis, Paper prepared for presentation at the Policy Responses to Unfettered Finance Workshop, North-South Institute Ottawa, Canada June 8–9, 2010. http://www.nsi-ins.ca/english/pdf/Canadian%20Banks%20(tony%20porter).pdf.

Quinn, G. (October 28, 2011). President Obama orders acceleration of technology transfer. http://ipwatchdog.com/2011/10/28/president-obama-orders-acceleration-of-technology-transfer/id=20060/.

RBA (Reserve Bank of Australia). (2011). Economic outlook, Reserve Bank of Australia. http://www.rba.gov.au/publications/smp/2011/feb/html/eco-outlook.html.

RBA (Reserve Bank of Australia). (August, 2012). Overview: Australia. http://www.rba.gov.au/publications/smp/2012/aug/pdf/overview.pdf.

Reavis, C. (2009). The global financial crisis of 2008–2009: The role of greed, fear and oligarchs, MIT Sloan Management Case #09-093, published 2009.07.22.

Reinhart, C. M., & Rogoff, K. S. (December 17, 2008). Banking crises: An equal opportunity menace. http://www.economics.harvard.edu/files/faculty/51_Banking_Crises.pdf.

Reinhart, C. M., & Rogoff, K. S. (2009). *This time is different: Eight centuries of financial folly*. Princeton: Princeton University Press. ISBN: 9780691142166.

Robertson, C. (n.d.). Canada, the USA, and the financial crisis: Risks and opportunities, Canada-US project at Carleton University. http://www.cdfai.org/PDF/Canada,%20the%20USA,%20and%20the%20Financial%20Crisis.pdf.

Schuler, D. (January 28, 2011). Why didn't Canada have a financial crisis? http://theglitteringeye.com/?p=12900.

Schwab, K. (Eds.). (2011). *The global competitiveness report 2011–2012*. Geneva: World Economic Forum.

Silva, D. (2009). Bank bailouts and the 2009 federal budget: The untold story of Canada's $ 275-billion financial bailout, in Financial meltdown: Canada, the economic crisis and political struggle, Relay a Socialist Project Review. http://www.socialistproject.ca/documents/FinancialMeltdown.pdf.

Taylor, F. (February 24, 2011). Australia economic outlook for 2011, Griffith University. http://www.franchise.edu.au/articles/Australian-economic-outlook-for-2011.html.

Taylor, C., Bradley, C., Dobbs, R., Thompson, F., & Clifton, D. (August, 2012). Beyond the boom: Australia's productivity imperative, McKinsey Global Institute. http://www.mckinsey.com/insights/mgi/research/asia/australia_productivity_imperative.

The National Bank. (July, 2012). Quarterly economic forecasts, The National Bank. http://www.nationalbank.co.nz/economics/forecasts/summary.aspx

The Japan Times (TJT). (July 10, 2013). IMF raises 2013 economic growth forecast for Japan: Revision reflects strong impact of monetary easing. The Japan Times, Business/Economy. http://www.japantimes.co.jp/news/2013/07/10/business/imf-raises-2013-economic-growth-forecast-for-japan/#.UeKtMSkVE0A. Accessed 14 July 2013.

The Treasury (New Zealand). (2013). New Zealand economic outlook: Moderate growth in New Zealand's economy expected to continue, The Treasury. http://www.treasury.govt.nz/budget/forecasts/befu2013/006.htm. Accessed 14 July 2013.

Treasurer. (April 21, (2009). Australia's policy response to the global financial crisis, Address to the Institute of Actuaries of Australia Biennial Convention 2009. http://www.treasurer.gov.au/DisplayDocs.aspx?doc=speeches/2009/011.htm & pageID=005&min=njs&Year=&DocType=.

Treasury. (2009). Economic and fiscal update overview, Budget Economic and Fiscal Update 2010, The Treasury Government Publication. http://www.treasury.govt.nz/budget/forecasts/befu2010/003.htm/.

Treasury. (2010). The economy of New Zealand: Overview, The Treasury Government Publication. http://www.treasury.govt.nz/economy/overview/2010/nzefo-10-2.pdf.

Treasury. (2012). Economic outlook, Budget Policy Statement 2012, The Treasury Government Publication. http://www.treasury.govt.nz/budget/2012/bps/10.htm.

Tripe, D. (2009). New Zealand and the financial crisis of 2008, Center for Banking Studies, Massey University. http://www.rbnz.govt.nz/research/workshops/june2009/3732339.pdf.

Wei, L. T. (March 9, 2009). Combating the global economic crisis: Japan's policies and politics, EAI Background Brief No.436. http://www.eai.nus.edu.sg/BB436.pdf.

Willis, B., & Liu, B. (January 9, 2012). U.S. economy's challenges greater this year than last, Gluskin Sheff says, Bloomberg. http://www.bloomberg.com/news/2012-01-09/u-s-economy-s-challenges-greater-this-year-than-last-gluskin-sheff-says.html.

World Bank. (January 18, 2012). Global economic prospects 2012a: Uncertainties and Vulnerabilities, World Bank Prospects. http://econ.worldbank.org/WBSITE/EXTERNAL/EXTDEC/EXTDECPROSPECTS/0,,contentMDK:23064688~pagePK:64165401~piPK:64165026~theSitePK:476883,00.html.

# Author Index




C. Y.-Y. Lin et al., *National Intellectual Capital and the Financial Crisis in Australia, Canada, Japan, New Zealand, and the United States*, SpringerBriefs in Economics, DOI 10.1007/978-1-4614-9308-2, © The Author(s) 2014

# Subject Index



C. Y.-Y. Lin et al., *National Intellectual Capital and the Financial Crisis in Australia, Canada, Japan, New Zealand, and the United States*, SpringerBriefs in Economics, DOI 10.1007/978-1-4614-9308-2, © The Author(s) 2014

# Subject Index

MIX
Papier aus verantwortungsvollen Quellen
Paper from responsible sources
FSC® C105338

If you have any concerns about our products,
you can contact us on
**ProductSafety@springernature.com**

In case Publisher is established outside the EU,
the EU authorized representative is:
**Springer Nature Customer Service Center GmbH**
**Europaplatz 3, 69115 Heidelberg, Germany**

Printed by Libri Plureos GmbH
in Hamburg, Germany